LIVING IN GOD WITHOUT GOD

LIVING IN GOD WITHOUT GOD

ROGER LENAERS, S.J.

CARYSFORT PRESS

A Carysfort Press Book
Living in God without God
by Roger Lenaers, S.J.

A translation by Dan Farrelly of *In Gott Leben ohne Gott* published by Edition Anderswo, Kleve 2015, which was translated from the Dutch *Al is er geen God-in-den-hoge*, Pelckmans, Kapellen, 2009

First published in Ireland in 2017 as a paperback original by
Carysfort Press, 58 Woodfield, Scholarstown Road
Dublin 16, Ireland

ISBN 978-1-909325-41-8

©2016 Copyright remains with the author
Typeset by Carysfort Press
Cover design by eprint limited
Printed and bound by eprint limited
Unit 35
Coolmine Industrial Estate
Dublin 15
Ireland

CONTENTS

PREFACE

The title may be surprising, even annoying. But it is necessary to know that it is a quotation from a letter dated 16 July 1944 and written by Dietrich Bonhoeffer from the Nazi prison in Spandau. In this letter he is tentatively formulating his fundamental intuition of a Christianity without religion which, in his view, ought to be the form of belief for the modern world. And then comes the sentence: 'Before God and with God we live without God.' Clearly, in this paradox the word 'God' is used in two different senses.

In 'without God' the name refers to the normal idea of God, namely, an almighty and omniscient person (in the Christian context even a three-fold person) in a second world above our own world. Out of that world this God intervenes at will in our world. He does this in the form of revelations, laws, miracles, and, depending on human behaviour, in the form of rewards or punishments. The existence of such a fundamentally anthropomorphic being is incomprehensible for modern people who have been exposed to the influence of the Enlightenment. Nothing speaks for it and almost everything speaks against it.

Bonhoeffer, too, rejects this idea of God which is that of the churches. But he rejects it for different reasons than those of modern humanism. In the Nazi period it became clear to him that this view of God fitted without any problem into a system which had no difficulty with wars of conquest, with national pride, human contempt, murder, violence, and repression. Did the churches see the contradiction between their idea of God and these forms of inhumanity? At any rate, they did not expressly distance themselves from this system, did not protest collectively, but rather, out of love for the fatherland, or out of fear, actively served the system. Bonhoeffer sees that such an image of God is to be rejected and that anyone who acts according to it is on the wrong track. This insight presupposes, of course, that he himself has an intuition of a more genuine idea of God; otherwise he would not have known that the false idea was false and he could not have rejected it with such decisiveness.

But what Bonhoeffer saw in a clear light only through his experience of Nazism had long since been there, indeed for many centuries. It is just that the Christians obviously did not notice anything suspicious. The inhumanity of Nazism was only the continuation of the hundreds of years of inhumanity right throughout the history of Europe. Faith in the Christian God-in-Heaven did not prevent pious Christians from continually waging war, with all the monstrous implications war involves; nor did they see any problem with the slave trade, with torture as a normal part of the justice system, with cruel executions adding to the people's amusement, with pogroms and witch hunts, with brutal intolerance. God-in-Heaven accommodated all of this, spreading his canopy over it, making it acceptable and sometimes even blessing it. As long as Christian society believed in this God-in-Heaven, i.e. up to the time of the Enlightenment, hardly any change was possible. And Christians believed in Him all this time because they could not see any salvation in this vale of tears without Him and because they thought it important to have Him as a friend in this life and even more in the transition to an afterlife; and also because they were afraid that He would not countenance their turning their back on Him, to say nothing of rejecting Him.

Only after the Enlightenment had knocked this God off His throne was there room for another, better image of God. Bonhoeffer saw this better image emerge from the Bible. The biblical Yahweh is also anthropomorphic and has the qualities and failings of a ruler, is warlike and biased, even sometimes cruel, which is the reason why Christians could consider such wrong attitudes to be not guilty or to be forgivable. But probably Bonhoeffer saw in the Bible above all the other image of God: His demand for truth and justice and His concern for mankind, qualities which already appear in the Old Testament and shine forth more brightly in the activity and words of Jesus. The image of God that Bonhoeffer saw was therefore the image of a God who is there for human beings and who calls on us to be human. In essence, it is the image of the God of modern believers. It is not yet systematically thought through by Bonhoeffer and is based on a one-sided reading of the Bible, the value of which must itself be critically examined. But, as to its content, the image can easily be built into a theologically-based modern image of God.

Then what does the image of God look like when it is both modern and Christian at the same time? It must include a rejection of everything that has to do with God-in-Heaven, the anthropomorphic ruler and law-giver and rewarder and punisher. And this is no easy undertaking, for the creed, the Bible, the liturgy, moral teaching, theology, Church history, canon law are full of this God-in-Heaven. The first chapter of this book will attempt a sketch of this new image of God. It is the image which Bonhoeffer refers to with 'before and with God', although he would perhaps not straightforwardly subscribe to the views put forward in this book. Possibly because he simply did not have the time to think through his intuition himself, for eight months after the letter he was hanged in Flossenburg.

In the modern image of God, and therefore in Bonhoeffer with his 'before and with God', God no longer means 'God-in-Heaven' but the profound spiritual depth of the cosmos of which we only see the surface. This depth is not a philosophical idea and is not some Thing. It is a loving spirit which takes shape in the cosmos which, gradually developing the man of the future, expresses and reveals itself in man. And this loving spirit says to man, the preliminary end stage of cosmic evolution, simply 'thou', and is Himself a 'thou'. The first chapter will deal with this more in detail.

The two-part expression in Bonhoeffer's 'before and with' is reduced in the title to the one word 'in'. This is because 'before and with' could give the impression of someone who observes us and co-operates with us from outside. Our actions, i.e. our ethics, should spring from the profound reality that is at work in us, to which we belong, through which we breathe and live, and which encompasses us from all sides. The preposition 'in' makes this clearer. It reminds us of the way in which Paul, in his letters, refers to his relationship with the living Jesus. The expression 'in Christus' occurs in Paul eighty times. What he is saying is that the consciousness of his link with the living Jesus Christ as it were envelops him, governs what he does and what he omits to do. This book is aimed at showing how the awareness of his unity with the loving spirit, who for Paul is the God and Father of Our Lord Jesus Christ, envelops, penetrates, carries, and defines the ethics of the modern Christian. The fundamental change of perspective that comes with modernity means also that this ethic will clearly distance itself in certain points from pre-modern ethics. In what points, and with what justification, will be dealt with in detail in what follows.

But 'living in God' includes more than the modern believer's ethics to which the present book is limited. 'Living in God' also includes a new kind of encounter with the fundamental wonder of God. We can call this encounter 'spirituality'. Here, the long revered Bible loses its status as a collection of infallible words uttered by God in Heaven and becomes words spoken by human beings, but of a particular kind, inspired, full of the spirit of God full of depth. The new image of God also influences prayer, with important consequences for the function and content of the liturgy, and especially for the sacraments, since liturgy and sacraments imply a role for God-in-Heaven, and the modern believer has taken his leave of this God. These themes are to be dealt with specifically in a separate book.

R.L.   Vorderhornbach
                                                        15 January 2017

CHAPTER ONE

Explanation of the Fundamental Idea of Modern Faith

In the letter of 16 July 1944 from the Nazi prison in Spandau to which the preface refers, Dietrich Bonhoeffer writes to his friend and later biographer Eberhard Bethge: 'We must live in the world as if there were no God – *etsi deus non daretur*. (...) God lets us know that we have to live as people who cope with life without God.' The Latin formulation was not his own. He was quoting from memory, and thus not quite accurately, a sentence of the Dutch Hugo Grotius. This Grotius (Hugo de Groot, 1583-1643), a Protestant lawyer and theologian, is one of the founders of modern international law. In his main work *De jure belli et pacis* (on law concerning war and peace) he maintains intuitively that natural law, on which international law is based, would still be in force *etiamsi daremus Deum non dari*, 'even if we were to suppose that there is no God.' Grotius was by no means aware of all the consequences of his intuition. Above all, he did not see that in this way he was, in fact, acknowledging the independence of the world from a law-giving Creator-God. For if natural law can stand even without God then God is not its creator, and if He is not its creator neither nature nor man (for natural law is human law, since only with regard to man is there a question of law) has anything to do with God-in-Heaven. They are not dependent on Him. They are, in other words, autonomous. This autonomy (Bonhoeffer calls it the maturity of man) also means that God cannot intervene and therefore is playing no role in human affairs. We therefore no longer need to concern ourselves with this God-in-Heaven. Bonhoeffer did foresee to some extent what far-reaching consequences Hugo Grotius's ideas would have for the modern Christian: namely, the end of the conviction, dominant until now, that above our world there is a higher world, a supernatural world, the result being a 'Christian a-theism'.

Three hundred years after Grotius this division was still the accepted colour filter through which the faithful in the West looked at reality. Bonhoeffer's theology was the first clear

rejection of this worldview. It was as if he opened the floodgates
of enlightened religious thinking. This new way for believers to
view reality poured with growing force into the church of the
West. Quite clearly, many no longer felt happy with the notions
of faith with which they had grown up. A sign of this was the
success in the 1960s of the book by the Anglican bishop John
Robinson: *Honest to God*. This book was, in fact, the forerunner
of a 'Christian atheism' in line with Bonhoeffer's thinking.

The present book aims at showing what such 'Christian
atheism' means in everyday life, i.e. what a modern Christian
ethic would look like. This new ethic is directly derived from a
modern form of believing. But this can only be clear to someone
who has the basic ideas of this modern faith clearly in mind.
Many readers may know too little about them or be unaware of
their implications. For this reason the fundamental ideas will be
sketched here. The clearer one's grasp of them, the clearer it will
become to what extent traditional ethical and religious notions,
to which people unconsciously cling, run counter to the
affirmation of these ideas. This paves the way for rethinking our
ideas, which is the purpose of this first chapter.

The pre-modern world view

The starting point is the fact that modern man, and therefore also
the modern Christian, sees reality quite differently from the way
it was seen in the past. People lived with the conviction that the
whole order of things is dependent on an almighty supernatural
world. This conviction was based on a combination of two
factors. The first factor is the human need for explanation and
security, whereas many natural phenomena seemed to be
completely inexplicable and made man aware of his inadequacy
and helplessness. But there was also a second factor at work: the
innate, subconscious, almost sleeping feeling that there is a
reality beyond us which encompasses everything but which
escapes and transcends us. The confrontation with phenomena
which are beyond our grasp and our control, awakened ever
anew this feeling, which therefore in the human consciousness
became closely associated with these phenomena, the result of
which was the conviction that in them powers surpassing us were
revealed. These powers were very real, but invisible and should

therefore belong to another realm, outside and above ours. Thus they became 'gods', invisible and immortal, but in other respects true copies of inner-worldly rulers. They inspired fear and demanded subservience and veneration. Why did primitive man locate their realm above, in the heavens? Probably because most of these phenomena, like thunder and lightning, hurricanes, solar eclipses, and comets came from heaven and also because the feeling of surpassing us, of transcendence, awakes automatically the idea of 'above'. Step by step man had made himself a clear image of this other powerful world. To this he had simply projected his own familiar human world up to that higher realm. Thus all that we say about what is 'above', comes from 'below'.

The inability to cope more or less reasonably with life led these mortals to look to forces outside the world for help. Obviously they vaguely knew that these forces were to some extent accessible, just like the rulers they had to deal with on earth. They also knew from experience how to win favour with these human rulers. They thought they could succeed in the same way with the heavenly powers: through petitions, eulogies, expressions of gratitude (sincere or otherwise), through bringing gifts (and thus sacrifices), through obedience to laws which they assumed came from on high, through self-punishment with a view to avoiding punishment from the powers above. The religions are nothing more than forms of veneration of these powers organized and conducted by specialists.

No wonder that the heavenly copy also shows most of the proprieties and deficiencies of the worldly original, even when man has tried to cleanse the copy to rid it of all the errors and failings of this original which are open to severe criticism. Even then the gods remained biased, unjust, merciless, venal, dangerous, dreadful.

The influence of minds that saw more deeply brought about, in the course of the centuries, a purification of the blameworthy faults and weaknesses of the human original. The result of it was the image of one god above, living in a world of light and justice, where there is no mortality, no suffering, no death; in a word, a perfect world. And because, up there, high above our heads, there is the expanse of the heavens, that world was given the name 'Heaven'. This perfect world rules, instructs, and rewards or punishes the doings of the mortals down here.

From such a perspective, miracles are not alien, just as today they are also completely unproblematic for a child. In the fairy tales a pumpkin can change into a carriage with four horses, if a fairy touches it with her magic wand, or the rock opens, when the right words are spoken. For that other world nothing is impossible. This pre-modern thinking can be termed *hetero-nomous*, for it sees our world and therefore also ourselves as completely dependent on the laws of that second world, and in Greek law is *nomos* and second *heteros*. In what follows, this way of thinking will often be referred to by the term heteronomous as well as by the terms pre-modern or supernatural.

The role of the Enlightenment

The 18th century came, and it brought about that crucial cultural change in the West which is called the Enlightenment. This Enlightenment was not a case of *generatio spontanea*. One can compare it with the appearing of a mushroom in autumn. The suddenly emerging mushroom is the product of an invisible web of nutrient threads that has developed for a long time in the soil. The Enlightenment can be traced back as far as the Renaissance and, from there, still further back into antiquity. The Renaissance was the mother of two typically Western achievements: human-ism and the modern sciences. The combined effect of these two had far-reaching consequences. First, the sciences narrowed down, more and more, the range of what was earlier inexplicable until there was hardly anything more of it left. Thunder and lightning, sickness and disease, good and bad weather, oracles and dreams, miracles, apparitions, clairvoyance, answering of prayers, stigmata – none of these had ultimately anything to do with intervention from a higher world. Everything was related to inner-worldly laws. The cosmos went along by itself. In other words, it was autonomous, for it found in itself (*autos*) the laws (*nomos*) it had to follow and did not dance to the tune of another world. Technology born from the sciences dealt with a whole range of vexations for which previously there had been no remedy. This lessened correspondingly the need for help from heaven. In the Middle Ages people had often referred to the world as a vale of tears, and rightly so. Thanks to the sciences and the technology born from them, this valley, while not yet changed into a paradise, sometimes gave the slight impression of paradise through the steadily increasing availability of medical care, means of communication, mobility, consumer goods, comfort and ease. This, then, led to man's not needing to beg God above to grant him well-being. A large part of this he could manage for himself. This brought an end to petitions, to the offering of sacrifice to appease the powers above, to the veneration of relics and saints so keenly practised in the Middle Ages.

The first factor in modernity (the modern worldview) is the consciousness of the autonomy of the cosmos awakened by the sciences; this autonomy means, even if that other world did exist, we hardly need it any more. The second factor, humanism, further reinforced this tendency. It seemed much more worthwhile and compelling to be preoccupied with humanity than with the heaven, which now seemed threadbare. Man was obviously a fascinating being, invested with inalienable rights, called to liberty, equality and (if he could manage it to some extent) fraternity. Briefly, he is no longer the poor being laden with guilt that the Middle Ages saw in him. The humanistic view, which since the Enlightenment had gained in tempo and conquered the West, freed him from this negative self-image. And what was true for the cosmos, namely, that it did not take orders from another world, had also to be true for man who had originated from the cosmos. He, too, did not have to accept laws from Sinai or from Vatican Hill. He should look for the laws within himself. He, too, was autonomous.

It is easy to guess the consequences. The Church, which considers itself as representative of the second world, saw its influence in Western society dramatically reduced. Its claims to the truth and its demand for obedience were listened to less and less. The branch on which it previously sat so securely began to crack in a frightening way. Now on the defensive Church leadership defended itself tooth and nail against the onslaught of 'unbelief', tried to erect dams to arrest the swelling flow of that unbelief, and showered powerless excommunications on the enemies of the Church. It was unfortunately blind to the values contained in the affirmation of the autonomy of cosmos and man. This rejection only made the situation worse for themselves. Modernity did not passively accept the unreasonable attack. It reacted with equal aggressivity. And because after the

Christianizing of Europe religion and Church were seen as identical, enmity towards the Church developed into enmity towards religion. The emergence of modern atheism is primarily the responsibility of the Church authorities, which were lagging behind and condemning modernity and its values.

The above has sketched the contrast between the worldview before the Enlightenment and the worldview that followed the Enlightenment, between heteronomous and autonomous thinking. But the good aspects of the one do not necessarily have to stand in the way of the good aspects of the other. Awareness of a holy transcendence as defended by heteronomous thinking fits easily together with the knowledge that man and cosmos are not hand puppets in a divine puppet theatre. A further explanation is needed as to how exactly the autonomy of man and cosmos are compatible and even inextricably linked with the reality of an unfathomable, nameless God.

God and the cosmos: a new view of creation

Today, when we use the traditional little word 'god', it should no longer refer to an almighty (and all-good) reality outside the cosmos, capable of intervening in earthly events at will. It should refer to the spiritual fundamental reality which transcends all things and expresses itself in the form of the cosmos, makes itself visible, reveals itself, and does this by means of evolution. This can be made clear by means of a comparison with a piano sonata of Mozart. This delightful cascading waterfall of sounds, i.e. of air vibrations, makes our ear drums vibrate, and these vibrations, after passing through the wonderful paths of the inner ear and the auditory nerve, are converted into electrical impulses which stimulate the brain and thereby become audible. Everything in this whole process can be described and explained scientifically, although even for science it remains a mystery how material stimuli can at the same time be conscious phenomena. However, the sonata is more than an exactly measurable series of vibrations in the air with varying frequencies. Through material vibrations it gives expression to a quite different kind of reality, namely, Mozart's inspiration. It is essentially the 'spirit' of Mozart embodied in matter, his inner self, which expresses its essence in this form of beauty. This spirit is not just an addition which scientific analysis could bring to light. Yet no one will call it nonsense if one were to speak here of inspiration, i.e. of spirit, nor would anyone think that acknowledging this spirit would amount to a threat to the scientific explanation of the musical phenomenon. The creative activity of the spirit does not intervene in the music from outside. It adds nothing to it and yet it is precisely what brings about and permeates the magical sound. This activity is its essential foundation and its ultimate explanation. The miracle of the sound is the spirit of Mozart himself which expresses itself in materiality. But self-expression of the spirit in materiality is precisely what we call creation. What the artist does is essentially this: he expresses his inner self in resistant matter. He reveals what lives in him and would otherwise remain inaccessible to others and even to himself.

Neo-Darwinism interprets the cosmic miracle as the result of the interplay between innumerable undirected mutations and natural selection throughout astronomically long periods of time. But it can also be interpreted as the self-revelation of a fundamental spiritual Wonder which gradually, in the evolution of living things, gives expression to ever more of its incomprehensible essence. If human creation of art is understood as self-expression of the spirit, the cosmos itself can also be conceived of as the result of such creativity. Creation is then no longer the 'making of something from nothing' to which an arid theology has reduced it. It is the progressive cosmic self-expression of a spirit that transcends everything. Thus it is possible, as a believer, to speak of creator and creation at the same time as retaining with the biology of evolution the full autonomy of the cosmos.

Furthermore, this interpretation casts light on several phenomena which in the mechanistic chance hypothesis remain a mystery. For example, that out of the non-conscious the phenomenon of consciousness could emerge. Indeed, to speak of a creative spirit is to speak of a completely conscious fundamental reality. In a preliminary first phase this spirit had to express itself in a purely material and therefore not yet conscious form. In the course of evolution this self-expression reached the level of animal consciousness and afterwards that of the human spirit. Obviously, a drive towards consciousness is embedded in the not yet living matter and reveals the active presence of a creative fundamental spirit. Mozart magnified to infinity. And at the same time purified from all the inadequacies present in all comparisons.

The biblical concept of creation also needs purification. It uses the language of comparison and is in danger both of opposing creator and cosmos in the way that we oppose a sculptor to his sculpture and of thus introducing the notion of two different worlds. Seeing in the cosmos the continually progressing self-expression of the transcendent spirit protects us from this error. This self-expression obeys all the laws discovered by the science of biological evolution: it follows the path of the continual sequences of mutations which improve each other in the course of inconceivably long geological periods. But this journey does not alter the fact that we are dealing with creation. For creation does not mean intervention from outside, but self-expression from within.

This conception is more deeply religious than the traditional one. The divine reality no longer dwells in another world. We encounter it in all that is, for everything is its self-revelation. This is the foundation for the self-evident need for reverence in dealing with nature and above all with human beings. Thus it also becomes clear that the divine fundamental reality strives to become man. This original Christian concept then takes on a meaning which is different from the traditional one. It no longer means that in a particular moment in cosmic history God comes down from heaven and becomes 'flesh'. It now means that the self-expression of God, the cosmos, is developing towards the emergence of the *species* man, and thus gradually becomes man.

This synthesis can be called *theonomy*, the term used by the German-American Paul Tillich, to say that the unfathomable/-incomprehensible reality which in Christian parlance is called 'God', in Greek *theos*, is the deepest reality and ultimate law (*nomos*) of the cosmos and of man. But *theonomy* is an unfortunate term. *Theos* has always pointed to a power outside the world, so that the adjective *theonomous* could likewise evoke a kind of *heteronomy*. Thus it is better to use the term 'modern believer', although this term offers no content with regard to the relation between faith and modernity. 'Inner-worldly' would be a useful synonym, but then the notion of transcendence is obscured. We shall continue using the three concepts inter-changeably.

So far, so good. And one could think that now all is clear. But theonomous thinking is autonomous thinking. Unfortunately, the whole formulation of the content of our faith is hetero-nomous from beginning to end, even when we are not aware of it. Fortunately, the above provides us with a simple criterion for separating the wheat from the chaff. As soon as we seek any clarification by recourse to intervention from outside the world we find ourselves operating with a pre-modern worldview. The same applies when we confess something which cannot be tested with inner-worldly means because it is supposed to be happening outside our world of experience. An example of the first case is 'the birth of Jesus of Nazareth from a virgin'; and of the second case 'that the world has been redeemed by the death of Jesus on the cross', or everything that is taught about expiatory sacrifice, indulgences, God's anger, Judgement Day. In both cases a different formulation or conception is absolutely necessary.

Following from the above is the crucial need to test the traditional content of Christian faith to ascertain its inner-worldly real value and, where it is found lacking in this respect, to give it a new formulation in language which is revelatory for modern man. Conservative believers will be up in arms against these new formulations. They do not see that formulations are time-related, even those which are thought to be expressions of eternal truths. They take something that is a provisional expression of truth in a particular cultural phase to be a defini-tive expression of reality and therefore just as unchangeable as divine reality itself. In this way they are making absolute divine statements out of inadequate human statements. In their eyes a new formulation is therefore *a priori* false, even heterodox.

A comparison with addition using a non-decimal number system shows up the short circuit in their thinking. In the binary system which has only the numbers 0 and 1 at its disposal, as is the case with digital addition, the sum of 1 and 1 is not 2 as in the decimal system, but 10. However, both results are equally correct. Everything depends on what numbering system is used. An equally clear comparison can be found in music. If the key of a melody is altered, so that a song written in C is transposed to E, no single note is the same as in the original song. And yet there is no change in the melody. In a similar way, nothing is lost of the life-enriching content of the early Church's belief in God and in Jesus if this content is expressed in new language. The content remains the same, yesterday as today. It is just that it is expressed in new words so as to be meaningful also today.

CHAPTER TWO

The Basis for a Modern Ethics for Believers

What we see determines what we do. Thus pre-modern modes of thinking are naturally followed by pre-modern modes of behaviour. Therefore in the Jewish-Christian culture the rules which govern our behaviour are from the beginning steeped in heteronomy. They are derived directly from the prevailing notions about the relationship between the cosmos and God. In this view of things all ethical laws come from above, from a divine law-giver. They are anchored there and find their ultimate justification there. We are not to bear false witness, 'because I am the Lord'. We have to honour father and mother, 'because I am the Lord'. We must not steal, 'because I am the Lord'. In Judaism all guidelines for life are to be found in the Torah. This word is usually translated as 'law'. But a better translation would be 'sacred teaching about life'. From this teaching the Rabbis have distilled 250 concrete commands and 365 concrete prohibitions which are meant to bring the life of the pious Jew in every tiny detail into line with the will of God. Christian culture did not simply accept this heritage, but limited it to the central core of the teaching – to the Decalogue, the so-called 'ten words'. This is the backbone of pre-modern ethics. This kernel was then enriched with elements taken from the New Testament. In the context of the further development of ethical sensitivity, Church leadership and its assistants, the moral theologians, treated these 'ten commandments' and the gospel extensions attached to them as if they were a framework of laws and supplied all kinds of practical applications. This is particularly evident in sexual ethics. If we ask in annoyance why a Jew cannot use a lift on the Sabbath or light a fire, we should also ask ourselves why in the past a Catholic should not eat anything before Communion or was not allowed to have sex in Lent. The answer is obvious: Church law forbids it, or the Rabbi says so, or it is the teaching of the Talmud. This human law interprets divine law and is there-fore sacred and unchallenged. But these are always directives coming from another world, given by the representatives of that other world and made more precise for the benefit of the ignorant people of this world.

The breakthrough of the Enlightenment was a kind of cultural mutation. This process needed about two hundred years, and the end result was a two-fold new insight. First, that Church teaching about another world, which could intervene at will in our world, found no confirmation or support in the world of our experience. Second, that all phenomena could be convincingly explained without recourse to that other hypothetical world. To prescribe behaviour or to justify its demands, the Church in the modern period can no longer appeal to commands originating from that other world. And it certainly no longer can when its prescriptions stand in the way of further human development, which in former times often was the case.

The birth of a new ethic

If what we see determines what we do, leaving behind the pre-modern worldview in favour of modernity has fundamental consequences with regard to ethics. If the holy power-line from heaven to earth, which was thought to travel via Vatican Hill, has been cut, the laws and prescriptions of our holy mother Church and of our Holy Father the Pope have had their time. This could look like liberation. The reality is that it means an arduous process of maturing. Previously believers could have confidence in the omniscience stemming from the other world, which through the mouth of the Church and the Pope taught them how they were to live. They needed only to comply. But in the 19th century this time came to an irrevocable end. No more pre-scriptions and guidelines were to be expected from that other world. It simply no longer existed. That had to have alarming consequences. All commands, the divine and the ecclesiastical, and the traditions and customs which grew out of them – in short, the whole secure organization of life for the individual and for society – had always derived their binding force from the conviction that they came from an omniscient God on High who watched carefully over their observance and would punish wherever the laws were flouted. Suddenly this God on High was no longer there. Neither were his laws. That had to lead to chaos

as in a country without police or law book or binding prescriptions. How was man to live in these circumstances? What
was still good and what was bad? Man could not seek guidance
from above, for that above had gone up in smoke. He had to find
it himself. To do so, he had finally to get rid of his immaturity,
become responsible, find his own way, search for the rules he was
to live by, within himself, dig them out of his own being. Because
that is where they lie hidden. Deep within himself there is a
thrust that drives him on and vaguely shows him the direction,
that of an incessantly progressing humanizing process. He is to
transcend the level of *homo sapiens* and become man as such.
Basically, he is still a 'missing link'. To fulfil this unclear task he
has reason and intuition at his disposal. And he can learn from
experience, through setbacks and successes. With the help of
these tools he is to find for himself what he must do and not do to
reach the ultimate goal to which evolution directs him.

Modern humanism has, in fact, been doing that. It has
developed an ethic without God or heavenly transcendence,
which focuses on the good of man as its central value. It has
chosen to work with the golden rule, which, formulated
negatively, says: 'do not do to others, what you would not wish
them to do to you', and not positively as the gospel requires: 'do
unto others as you would wish them to do to you'. For a positive
formulation it went instead to Kant: 'Act as everyone might be
allowed to act in the same circumstances.' This formulation is
very abstract and has no particular content. On the other hand, it
is broad enough also to encompass the sphere which does not
deal directly with relationships between people, which is where
the golden rule applies. For example, 'be the person you are, live
creatively, not as a consumer, don't follow the wind of every
fashion, watch your diet, avoid addictions.' In this way this new
ethic integrates much more clearly than does traditional ethics
the whole sphere of culture. Culture is precisely what gradually
distinguishes us from animals and is therefore typically human.
This view, which is still too one-sidedly focused on man, was
subsequently enriched by humanism, on the basis of man's
essential link with nature, with the duty of concern with the
environment, with protection of the rain forests, and with
keeping our ecological footprint small. The ethics of modern
humanism thus includes also protection of animals. For Christianity of the past, protection of the environment and of animals

were unknown concepts. It was blind to the miracle that each animal and each tree is.

Farewell to pre-modern ethics

One might well have expected that the ethics of humanism, despite leaving behind belief in revelation, would not remove itself a long way from pre-modern ethics. Modern humanism is, after all, basically the late fruit of Christian humanism. It has grown in the soil of a thousand years of Christianity. This can clearly be seen if Western ethics is compared with the thinking of Islam. Although this has many points of convergence with that of Christianity, it is nevertheless quite different. Having grown on Arabic soil, under the influence of Judaism and Christianity it did abandon Arabian polytheism, but ethically it travelled a different road from that espoused by the gospel. Precisely for this reason Islam lacks those elements which are characteristic of modern humanism, such as religious freedom, tolerance, rejection of violence, equal rights for women, respect for the physical integrity of the person, social lawgiving. The fact that in humanist ethics shared humanity is a central value is due to the gospel having paved the way. Indeed, in the course of time gospel ethics developed, in a humanistic way, the traditional 'Ten Commandments'. Of course, it must be admitted that it took about 1500 years before the slumbering seeds began their powerful growth. But from the very beginning, a humanistic tendency was intrinsic to the Christian interpretation of the 'Ten Commandments'. As early as the year 55, Paul of Tarsus wrote succinctly and forcefully in his letter to the Galatians that the whole Torah is summed up in the one phrase: 'Love thy neighbour as thyself.' With these words he paraphrased what Jesus said, that 'the whole Torah and the prophets are based on the commandment of love'. These words of Jesus and Paul clearly reveal the humanistic content which they saw rooted in the Torah.

This content did not come from Jesus or Paul but from the authors of the Torah. In the laws of the so-called Book of the Covenant which, in the book of Exodus follows the promulgation of the 'Ten Commandments', the humanistic aspect is often apparent. We even find reference to love of one's enemy, which is always considered to be of exclusively Christian heritage. On the other hand it must be admitted that this humanist character is missing from many laws in the Book of the Covenant. Several quite clearly contradict some of the human rights which are now considered inviolable. Thus the law of the talion: 'An eye for an eye, a tooth for a tooth' does not acknowledge the right to physical integrity. Mosaic law also, without reservation, permits slavery, thereby denying the right to personal freedom. And, as is still the case in Islam, the death penalty is treated as normal in the Torah, even with considerable inhumanity in its execution, as with death by stoning or even by burning at the stake.

Because of these inhumane elements human rights were for a long time obscured also in the Christian world, for the Old Testament was always regarded as just as holy and just as directly inspired by God as the New Testament. This was partly due to the pre-modern view that the scriptural word and the word of God were the same, which came from a lack of historical criticism. But only partly. This identification suddenly stopped in the practical sphere when Christians let themselves be led by a corrupt concern for their survival as a social group – whether it be the Church, their own people, the tribe, the family – and simply ignored some very humanistic words of the Scriptures. How else could the cruelty of the mediaeval justice system be reconciled with the explicit demand to practise mercy, which is everywhere in the New Testament? Or how could the thousand-year-long European anti-Judaism be reconciled with the Pauline hymn to the Jewish people in the Letter to the Romans 11:28-29? Or how could there be discrimination against women despite the statement of complete equality of man and woman in the letter to the Galatians 3:28? Or the continual wars which have bloodied European history, despite the recurring refrain that God is a God of peace? Are these texts suddenly no longer to be seen as the 'word of God'?

Despite the incontrovertibly humanistic quality of the Jewish-Christian ethics, which also cannot be diminished by the above criticism of the Book of the Covenant, the ethics of modern humanism has, in a relatively short period of time, become quite distant from it in several areas. The refusal of the European Parliament in 2007 to accept Rocco Buttiglione as Commissioner for Justice is an example of this. In the screening process for this position Buttiglione failed as a candidate because on this occasion he condemned homosexuality as sinful. In the Christian camp this outcome was seen as a hidden persecution of the Church. But what really became evident here was the gap between a heteronomous and an autonomous world view and ethic, and the mutual lack of understanding. The believer should try to appreciate the feeling of estrangement experienced by most of the representatives, when they heard the word 'sin' and how uncomfortable it must have been for them. 'Sin', surely, is a concept which belongs exclusively to the religious language of the past. It treats particular human behaviour as a violation of a law of God-in-Heaven, who will punish the guilty party for it, if not now then definitely in the other world. Modern man feels, when confronted with this view of things, as if he is being transported into a mythical, unreal world, as if someone is defending in all seriousness the existence of a world of goblins and elves, and derives from it binding rules of behaviour for human society. If Buttiglione had used the term 'sin' in reference to a child molester and murderer like Dutroux perhaps the parliament would have let it go. But he used the term in order to label as guilty, on the authority of an other-worldly law-giver, behaviour which modernity on the basis of its humanistic worldview finds understandable. And this happened although Bottiglione had already poured water into his pre-modern wine. While for his condemnation of homophilia he did use the Bible as a basis, under the influence of the climate of modernity he no longer defended the death penalty which would have been the Old Testament punishment for that misdeed.

And by the way, on the basis of the Bible, Christianity for centuries really did punish homophilia with death. They did this very consistently, much more consistently than was the case with Rocco Buttiglione, who in no way argued in favour of such a punishment. What a furore would he have unleashed if for biblical reasons he had done that! But he was himself not in agreement with the death penalty, although the divine law of the Torah (if only with a single verse) required it. He himself felt this demand was an error. And so, God's word is an error? Here we can see how even the defenders of heteronomy have absorbed, without realizing it, much of modern-thinking culture. Clearly the groundwater of modern thinking has slowly seeped even into the cellars of the Vatican. No wonder, when the whole Western world is under water.

Humanism that has high ethical values and has parted company with the God-in-Heaven can be something very noble, but it has manifested, deep within it, a chasm of inhumanity. Both Marxism and Nazism are products of a humanism which proclaims the death of God. Together they are responsible for the millions of sacrifices under the regimes of Hitler, Stalin, Mao and Pol Pot. The inhumanity born of atheistic humanism is no less than what the thousand years of the Christian Middle Ages and Counter Reformation have on their account. And that is no small tally. However, that should not close our eyes to the good that humanist ethics has brought about, for otherwise we would be committing the reverse of the same error made by the embittered opponents of Christianity, who, in settling their account with the Church, seem only to see the bad in it.

In search of a modern ethic for believers

The pre-modern ethics we drank in with our mother's milk has obviously served its time in the Western world. Anyone who cannot accept the ethics of modern humanism because of its potentially destructive tendencies, but is just as unable to believe any longer in the traditional ethics, has to look for a third way. This has to be a modern way which takes human autonomy seriously but which is also at the same time a possible route for believers, one which achieves the closest possible connection with the fundamental divine Mystery, seen with the eyes of Christian faith. We need, therefore, an ethics for believers which has a different foundation from that of the traditional one and which therefore has some different elements of content. On the one hand, it should find its inspiration in the gospel, and on the other hand, it should plainly acknowledge the autonomy of the cosmos and of man. This ethics rejects just as resolutely as does modern humanism the existence of a prescriptive, controlling and punishing law-giver in an almighty supernatural world. It therefore resolutely denies that that authority would have a legitimate mouthpiece on earth like the religious rulers in Teheran, Mecca or Rome, empowered to decide what is good and what is bad. This is the way the modern believer sees it. He does not find in an infallible book what he has to do or not to do, nor does he hear it from an infallible teaching authority. He looks for it where it should be found, namely, in the essence of man. In this way the content of the modern believer's ethics largely coincides with that of the modern humanist. But the ultimate responsibility and motivation for what both groups read from the essence of man with regard to what is good or bad, will be different. Their view of the essence of man is different and must result in differences of content. The differences between their views on euthanasia and abortion have their origins here.

What, therefore, are their different views of human essence? For the modern humanist man is the product of a directionless and therefore blind cosmic evolution. In this view every form of planning is denied. The whole process of cosmic development which has led to the emergence of the human species is, in this view, pure chance, without any intrinsic meaning. However, humanity is simply there, and we belong to it, and it makes its demands on us. For example, the demand to accept one another as we are, because only on this condition is living together possible and fruitful. Also the need to work together to prevent disaster or to repair any damage that has been suffered. And oddly enough, in doing this we experience something like meaning in this universe which of itself is 'meaningless'.

By contrast, the Christian considers man as a wonder which results from the spiritual fundamental Reality which produces all things and which strives for an ever richer self-expression. A Christian ventures to interpret the essence of that spiritual fundamental Reality using the human category love. Our impulse to love our fellow men and to cultivate all that has human value arises therefore from a much richer source than the one seen in the modern humanist view. It is not rooted in chance, and it is not without direction, but is rooted in the absolute. The ethical impulse owes to this origin the absoluteness which characterizes all its ethical demands.

However, the differences in content between the modern humanistic and modern believer's ethics are not derived primarily from their different attitude with regard to trans-cendent reality. Some do. For example, that the humanist does not pray, but the Christian does. The Christian finds prayer important for his human development because it links him with God, the fundamental Mystery which is the foundation of his existence. For the humanist, on the other hand, a fundamental Mystery which is supposed to have produced us is pure fantasy.

What the believer calls 'praying' is in the eyes of the humanist only a kind of self-reflection or an attempt to telephone the man in the moon.

But most of the differences in content originate from their different relationship to Jesus of Nazareth. The Christian sees in him the concrete manifestation of what God, the fundamental Mystery, wants to achieve: his achieved human self-expression. This definitely provides a direction. Having something concrete, a model, is always a valuable aid to finding and following the right path. The inspiration which comes from the model which the Christian sees in Jesus of Nazareth leads to the most sublime human forms of behaviour not yet attained by modern humanism. Take, for instance, Jean Vanier, who began with the foundation of the 'Arche' and whose enterprise is continued by like-minded people who, day and night, live together with mentally disabled persons. Or the care within Church communities of people sick with leprosy. Or what Sister Emmanuelle has done in taking part in the life of the people who rake through the mountains of rubbish in Cairo and in trying to improve if only a little their degrading living conditions,. Or what Mother Theresa has achieved. Active love for fellow men has been much more in evidence in the Christian camp than in that of modern humanism.

The two forms of the one Christian ethics

The ethics of the modern believer is distinct not only from the humanistic but also from the traditional ethics housed in the Church. Both may be equally Christian and may have the same roots. However, there is a clear distinction between them. The consequences for ethical praxis will be dealt with in more detail in Chapter Three, but the very different orientation of the two should first be clarified here.

For the pre-modern believer the ethical imperative seems to come to man from outside. God-in-Heaven does not only reveal truths to be believed which we would otherwise not find out about, but He approves of particular kinds of behaviour, even requires them, as with the Ten Commandments. There are others which are at least recommended, like the evangelical counsels which find their place in monasteries. Other things are forbidden and punished, like birth control and homosexual relationships, and that makes them ethically bad. In this conception of things the ethical quality of behaviour is not determined by any kind of inner logic, namely by reference to the demands of human nature, which wants to become more perfect, but by a super-natural command or prohibition. In the case of the contra-ceptive pill Pope Paul VI did try to argue from natural law imbedded in man by God. Here he was close to the fundamental principle of the humanists. But ultimately he derived his prohibition of artificial birth control from the will of God. The same applies to the prohibition of homosexual activity. If the Torah and still more the epistle to the Romans had not con-demned this activity so absolutely, the Church's resistance to it would have been less noticeable. Ethically good behaviour, in this system, is obeying the laws which God-in-Heaven through the biblical authors has revealed to man. Pre-modern ethics is essentially law-based ethics.

The logical conclusion is that God, in His sovereign wisdom, could also have made quite other decisions. He could, for example, have allowed polygamy or even preferred it to monogamy; or He could have approved of slavery (and the Old Testament criticized neither the one nor the other) or the persecution and extermination of unbelievers to the greater glory of God – which the prophet Elijah in 1 Kings 18:40 zealously did with 450 priests of Baal. God is not bound by anything and needs to take nothing into consideration in what He does. In no case does He need to take heed of what men would like to be done. If human ideas or sensibilities should have played any role in His decisions He would have ceased to be God-in-Heaven, the absolute and sovereign judge.

The fundamental weakness of such an ethics, based on law, is its inability to stand up to critical reason. Take two examples from the sphere of sexual ethics. The Church has always strictly condemned pre-marital intercourse. It was a mortal sin and led to punishment in hell. But something which only a few hours before the official marriage was a mortal sin was, a few hours after it, virtuous. The same human act carried out with the same feelings and experiences surely cannot transform itself in the course of a few hours into its ethical opposite. A second example: one who marries again after a divorce is, according to the Church's ideas on morality, as long as the first partner is still alive, a public sinner. If the first partner has the good idea of dying, the mortal sin can be changed in a flash into virtue without the slightest change in the person in question. The only change – and this has surely no ethical aspect – is that another subject has breathed his last.

The ethics of a modern believer will derive its norms and judgements from the essence of man. In this it does not differ from the ethics of the humanist unbeliever. It will also be able to stand up to criticism. But in this view man is essentially a spark of an absolute fundamental love which reveals itself step by step and seeks to express itself ever more clearly. Thus there is in man a fundamental drive to continue to grow existentially by going out of himself, concerning himself with his fellow men, allying himself with them, being conciliatory and showing mercy – precisely by loving. The ethics of the modern believer is an ethics of love. It follows that what is born of love is by the same token ethically good and that nothing which is contradictory to love can ever be called ethically good or imposed or even tolerated. In view of this it is unthinkable that God on High could issue prescriptions by which respect for man or woman would ever be trampled underfoot. And if any human authority, even a religious one like the Iranian guardians of faith, or a Church authority like the Vatican, should in the name of God command or justify such actions, a modern believer should oppose it. And if out of fear of the consequences one did not dare to do it openly (remember the means which the Inquisition had at its disposal – not everyone has the blood of martyrs in his veins) one should at least not stop inwardly saying 'no'.

The concrete content of a modern believer's ethics will thereby clearly, but not essentially, differ from that of a pre-modern ethics. The God in the depths of us who urges us to love is none other than the God-in-Heaven who lays down laws. In principle, His laws will have the same aim as has the love of our fellow man, which tells us within ourselves what we should do and what we should not do. However, the transition from an ethics dictated from another world to an ethics based on this world means great progress. As will be seen in the next chapter, there are great deficits in the pre-modern, otherworldly ethics. For the Church, which is called to serve the well-being of man and to promote his further human development, this transition is extremely important.

Chapter Three

The Pre-Modern Law-Based Ethics

What are the deficits of pre-modern ethics? In other words, why is a law-based ethics which calls on God-in-Heaven, despite its undoubted merits, little more than a pair of crutches which mankind had to use for the time being, a phase in human development which was to be passed through and left behind? A critical analysis of the nature of law-based ethics can make this clear. The weaknesses which such an analysis will bring to light are typical of every kind of law-based ethics, and therefore of a religious and biblical one or of that of the Sharia. These deficits make it clear that it is an error to expect ultimate salvation from unwavering loyalty to something that has been prescribed. This holds equally for divine and ecclesiastical laws.

Every law-based ethics is the work of human beings

The first great weakness of laws which are thought to be divine is that they are formulated by human beings. Even if one believes in a completely just world up above, imperfect human intermediaries are necessary to receive whatever messages come from on high and to put them into words – prophets, shamans, seers, sibyls, oracles. These intermediaries have their own sensitivities, prejudices and limitations. And their share of blindness. And a portion of malice. Perhaps not a very great portion, but still large enough for the so-called divine will not to come through to us in its purity but mixed with the ideas, desires and preferences of the intermediaries. And these latter belong also to an impure culture which is reflected in them. Thus in the scriptures which are considered sacred there are utterances of aggressiveness, nationalism, worship of riches and power. Islam does not accept this with regard to the Koran. The words of Allah communicated to Mohammed by the angel Gabriel would have gone through Mohammed as through unblemished crystal. The history of Mohammed's life or the Arabic culture to which he belonged would not have had the slightest influence. Of course, that cannot be the case for him any more than for any other human intermediaries. The aggressiveness and the instinct for self-preservation which are in us from our animal pre-history result in the transcendent power – the working of which we experience in ourselves – taking the form of a warlike god. What in fact happens is that man deifies and justifies his own desire to fight, making this desire into the god of war Mars, or Ares and turning even the Bible's Yahweh into a god of war, a Lord of hosts, as in the case of the (by the way, not historical) conquering of the Promised Land. In this way man sanctifies war and power politics. Just as with Islam, Christianity has no clean slate. We have only to think of the crusades and the wars of religion. Blaise Pascal once said that people never act badly with such thoroughness and joy as when they act with religious conviction. The naturalness with which the Christian West waged war over the course of a thousand years must have to do with this. The Bible shares responsibility for the eager approving of the endless cases of murder and destruction which characterizes the history of Christian Europe. The aggressiveness in the not yet purified hearts of many biblical authors is visible in their writings, and their idea of God has the hue of blood. And this (which applies likewise to the image of Allah in the Koran) encouraged the acceptance of power politics, war and patriotism at the expense of other peoples. The consequence was that the different kind of message brought by Jesus could hardly make itself heard and that therefore one catastrophe after another has afflicted the world.

Four other weaknesses in pre-modern law-based ethics

The second weakness of every law-based ethics, and therefore also of pre-modern Christian ethics, is that every law leaves open a back door through which one can escape observance of the law without being considered a law-breaker. This can be seen with every man-made law. Without infringement of the law which requires payment of appropriate taxes one can use all legal possibilities so cunningly that one ends up paying much less tax than one should, or even none at all. Or one can cleverly draw out a lawsuit for such a long time that it lapses – the statute of limitations applies and one escapes the fine which was justly incurred. Such tricks can also be used with regard to the laws of the law-giving God. Matthew 15:5-6 is an example of this. Jesus severely condemns the trick of declaring one's possession *korban*, i.e. a present to the temple, with a view to escaping the sacred duty of providing financially for one's needy parents. If anything was *korban* it was to remain in the possession of the owner until his death so that he could bequeath it in its entirety to the temple. In a system of ethics based on love of mankind such unethical behaviour is unthinkable. The fact that a law-based ethic which appeals to Scripture leaves open such escape routes is also linked with the fact that the conceptions and sensitivities of the many biblical authors are different and, correspondingly, so is the way in which they formulate their message or inspiration. In the Old Testament we can often find praise of riches as a sign of Yahweh's blessing. In the New Testament, on the other hand, the rich man has as much difficulty entering the kingdom of God as the camel has of passing through the eye of a needle. Texts of the first kind are excellently suited to escape from the unpleasant demands of the second kind. That explains why Christians have no problem, despite 'blessed are the poor' and 'woe to the rich' (which, incidentally, can also be heard in the words of the Old Testament prophets), with eagerly serving Mammon. This is what people prefer to do. And what we prefer to do is what we do more readily. Hence the gigantic gulf between wealthy countries of the Christian West and the degrading poverty of the Third World. As with the justification of war, the biblical authors have unconsciously abetted a mixture of the divine message with an all-too-human acquisitiveness and have in this way weakened in Christians their sense of justice.

The third weakness in every law-based ethical system is that the formulation of the law must always remain more or less general. It is essentially a rule for the greatest possible number of cases and cannot deal with all conceivable and inconceivable cases and take into account all exceptions to the rule. There would be no end to it. An example: on the Sabbath, the Bible teaches in a general way, no work is to be done. But what counts as work and what does not? And so, what does the divine law allow and what does it not allow? The Scripture explicitly names certain things. It is not permitted, for example, to gather wood on the Sabbath. According to Numbers 15:35 the guilty person is even to be stoned to death. Similarly, according to Exodus 35:3 it is not permitted to light a fire. The Bible does not mention a whole host of other activities. Here begins the role of the interpreter, who, however, is a person with his own sensitivities and preferences even if in the eyes of the community of believers he is a mouthpiece of God. This expert decides about what can be done on the Sabbath without profaning it. Thus it is permitted to pull one's ox out of a ditch, as we can see from Luke 15:5, which is clearly a much bigger task than picking up wood or lighting a fire. In this way man becomes dependent on the will of other fellow human beings, whereas he should be listening to the transcendent law within him.

A fourth weakness is that the laws are relative to their time. A law has as its aim to achieve order in the life of a society at a particular time and in a particular culture. Thus the evolution of cultures continually requires new additions and corrections. The human law-giver can undertake these at any time. But divine laws are fundamentally unchangeable. If He were to change His laws God would be admitting that they had not been properly thought through. At most He can afterwards clarify the laws to some extent. Besides, with the completion of the Bible he can no longer even do that. According to tradition, revelation ended with the death of the last apostle. Since then, the best we can do is, in our daily lives, to 'tinker with' what was written down at God's bidding. Church laws, on the other hand, are not unchangeable and the Church leadership can therefore revise them, and does so occasionally. But it has the tendency to think that some of its laws are to some extent divine laws and are therefore unchangeable. Here one can think of the exclusion of women from ecclesiastical offices or the refusal of communion to people who have married again. Jewish casuistry offers a whole host of examples of this. Is El-Al permitted to fly on the Sabbath? To answer this question the biblical scholar searches in the biblical prescriptions and prohibitions for something which could, with much good will, be applicable to the problem of air travel. In this way the so-called will of God is like wax in the hands of a specialist, who shapes it according to his own lights and afterwards presents the result as the will of God.

A fifth weakness is the necessarily limited compass of a law book, whereas the process of humanization incessantly brings with it new ethical demands. For this reason even a divine law-giver could not provide a written veto against much that we do, even when it harms our growth as human being and fellow human being. But to convince oneself that everything that is not explicitly forbidden by the law-giver is permitted, opens the gates to many forms of cheating. In addition to this, a law formulated 2,000 years ago in a different cultural situation cannot possibly forbid something which only much later emerged as reprehensible and therefore to be absolutely forbidden. Belonging to this category, for example, are torture, sadism, slavery, the death penalty, cruelty to animals, intolerance. Or all the abuses which are only made possible by modern technology and liberal capitalism. In this way great ethical vacuums are automatically created in law-based ethics. In these vacuums we can without scruples give free rein to our desires, even if they involve contempt for mankind, because they do not contravene any explicit divine prohibition.

But the majority of our deeds by far are not covered by divine laws. The Rabbis may have distilled 250 commands and 365 prohibitions from the Torah, and Church leaders may then have decreed an abundance of laws, but there are thousands of actions about which absolutely nothing is said. Is it ethically acceptable to take part in games of chance, like the lotto, where large winnings are played for? Is it permissible for me to allow myself a luxury holiday in the Maldives? Am I allowed to threaten a suspect with torture (only threaten!) to force a confession from him? Is it my duty to participate in this protest rally or that signature campaign? Am I allowed to smoke in the knowledge that it is harmful to my health and disadvantageous to my fellow men? Is it right for me to watch television programmes in which violence seems to be the most normal thing in the world? Should I not do something to counter my being overweight? Does my addictiveness to sports coverage remain within tolerable limits? One can search through the whole Bible and the whole codex of canon law without finding an answer to such questions. Do these things therefore have nothing to do with ethics, which is surely the concrete formulation of what our human development requires of us? On the contrary, our human development depends even primarily on the answers we give to these everyday questions. This shows indirectly that a God-in-us, who continually urges us to further human development, penetrates and enriches our lives more intensively and more lastingly than the law-giving God of pre-modern times. This God is encountered only at particular moments, namely, when one disobeys His prescriptions, especially His ritual prescriptions, or His prohibitions. By contrast, in the inner-worldly system I encounter the creative fundamental Love, the true God, every time I ask myself whether what I am doing is useful or harmful to my fellow man or the environment. This question is posed by love, which is God's presence in me and which wants to increase further.

A sixth and final great weak point: no law without punishment

The sixth and perhaps most fundamental weakness in the earlier system of ethics is the essential link between law and punishment. A law without sanctions to enforce it is nothing more than a scarecrow. It is essential that it be supported by punitive measures. We too obey certain prescriptions less out of concern for the common good than out of fear of being caught. Where a speed sign on the road says 50 and there is hardly any traffic and we do not see why we should not drive at 80 or 100, we will duly drive at 50 so as not to be caught speeding and fined. And the law against driving with more than 0.5 m/l prevents many a person from drinking a few more glasses: one could be breathalysed on the way. People clearly do not conform to these limiting prescriptions out of concern for the safety of others on the road. When it comes to observing the law only appreciable penalties are effective. We know this from experience. Clearly, humanity still reacts childishly and immaturely. The same applies to us. In a humanity which has not yet reached maturity punishment seems to be the only means to make it clear that the law is something important, not a joke but a great good for each and every one of us. Anyone who abuses this good should be made to realize it in his own body: he will be punished, a penance will be imposed on him, he will be deprived for a while of the freedom which is so dear to him; in days of old (and still, in the Sharia) he would be whipped, his hand would be cut off, he would be sent to the gallows; things would be done to him which he was right to be afraid of. This procedure is not essentially different from the training of animals. But animals are precisely

not human beings and cannot act ethically. They obey
conditioned reflexes which we produce in them with the aid of
punishment and reward. Treating people like animals does not
promote their ethical growth, but keeps them back at what is still
a pre-human level. It has to be said, with Immanuel Kant, that
fear hollows out the ethical quality of our actions, their capacity
to promote our own spiritual growth and that of society. Acting
without concern for the common good but only to avoid
punishment and therefore out of self-interest, does not promote
human development and has therefore no ethical value. Looked
at from this angle, law-based ethics is a second-rate ethics. If
human development is sacred to us – and evolution and ultimately the God who is at work in it have this development as
their aim – it is wise to drop it in favour of an autonomously
orientated ethics.

As long as the Church leadership had power within this world
it could impose real and very painful punishments for offences
against divine and Church law. Everyone was aware of it, and
that made people behave. Out of fear. Perhaps this was the only
way Church authorities could enforce observance of their laws.
But ultimately was not more lost than gained by this?
Fortunately, the Church no longer has this arsenal of punitive
measures at its disposal. And even then it could not punish
everything, for example, inner sins, as in those against the ninth
commandment. In this case it was left to the judge in the other
world who sees everything, does not look away, and punishes.
Experience teaches us, however, that seldom does anything come
of punishment in *this* world. Those who deserve punishment
often do very well and those who should be rewarded often do
very badly. Punishment must then happen in the other world, in
the sphere of God-in-Heaven. But if the laws come from a second
world and are only punished in that world, a pre-modern
Christian ethics no longer has a future in a society which has
taken its leave of that second world. In such a society a network
of laws can perhaps maintain social order, which is indispensable, but it fails miserably when it comes to promoting true
human development.

The relationship between an ethics of love and a law-based
ethics can well be compared with the relationship between the
circumference of a circle and the rectangle drawn inside it. One
can increase the number of the sides of this rectangle a thousand-

fold in the hope that the rectangle will finally coincide with the circumference. As we know, this hope is illusory. Even in a rectangle with ten thousand sides, after meeting the circumference the sides are again distinct from it. Just as illusory is the idea that thanks to an ever greater increase in the number of laws and prescriptions (think of the c. 2,000 paragraphs in the Codex of Canon Law) human law will in the long run coincide with the will of God. For God is love. The circle is the image of an ethical attitude which is led not merely repeatedly but continually by the deepest law of our being, which is love. The difference between the two can be illustrated also by reference to the text of Galatians 5:1-6 about the insufficiency of observance of the Torah by comparison with belief in Jesus. What is meant by this faith is that one accepts being led by the spirit of Jesus. Whoever does this comes to the Father, and 'Father' is Jesus' own symbolical language for the fundamental Reality which produces and moves everything forward and which we can call ultimate Love and God.

Pre-modern ethics comes into conflict with human autonomy

The foregoing analysis makes it clear that law-based ethics cannot be the last word. But it comes under still heavier fire if our starting point is the central belief of modern thought that human dignity and essential human rights are absolute and inviolable. It has always been known that man has rights. But they always used to be limited rights which were dependent on decisions of higher powers: tribe, guild, community, prince, state, Church. As yet one did not have rights simply as a human being. One had rights when the prince bestowed them or because one belonged to a group or society which had acquired rights. And ultimately all rights came from God-in-Heaven who communicated them through His representatives on earth, whether secular or religious. The Enlightenment made it clear that man has rights simply by virtue of being man, and that these rights are absolute. 'Absolute' contains the idea that nothing, not even a divine command, can justify the failure to recognize these rights.

The forerunner of this awareness was Hugo Grotius, but the first official declaration of such rights came with the beginning of the French Revolution on 26 August 1789 under the name of *La déclaration des droits de l'homme et du citoyen*. About 150 years later, on 10 December 1948, the UN issued the *General Declaration of Human Rights*, although at the time it was not yet signed by the Soviet Union, the USA and ... the Vatican State. As long as the Vatican keeps to its pre-modern thinking, it cannot honestly be a signatory. In pre-modern thinking God alone has absolute rights. And so the Church authorities stubbornly opposed the doctrine of the absolute nature of human rights.

And even in the plans for the Second Vatican Council produced by the Curia at the Vatican the right to freedom of conscience was branded a pernicious error. Man has only the rights which God, his Lord, bestows on him. But freedom of conscience, namely the right of man to decide for himself which religious and ethical values are important to him, was not given to him by God. For He has clearly said what man has to think and to believe, namely what His Church says is to be believed. God is no more bound by the rights of man than by the laws of nature. He can therefore give commands and orders which entirely contradict the declaration of human rights accepted by the UN. In the Bible there is a whole host of examples of such commands. As long as the Church authorities had the requisite indispensable power it followed this example and punished accordingly any behaviour which did not conform. And indeed, not just such behaviour but even thinking which was clearly out of line. What else was the crime of the so-called heretics which they combatted with fire and sword?

Such punishments were approved by the faithful foot-soldiers or at least were not condemned by them. Since the Lord God is the highest wisdom and the Church authorities have a modest share in His wisdom, their commands were also wise commands, however harsh they could occasionally be. On the basis of this conviction the theology of the time was able to prove that even such ecclesiastical prescriptions and demands, which later were unmasked as a blasphemous abuse of power and pilloried by the world's conscience, were pleasing to God and necessary. And over everything that had become law and custom in Christian society – the Greek *nomos* has both meanings – the hetero-nomous ethics stretched a heavenly canopy and thus protected it from human criticism. It is only too clear how much this attitude had to be prejudicial to the growth of genuine humanity.

This heavenly canopy also explains how it comes about that in the papal documents in the Middle Ages or in the writings of the great scholastic theologians and fathers of the Church like Thomas Aquinas and Bonaventura there were no protests or arguments against slavery or the slave trade or against war (on the contrary: 'It is God's will!' was the motto of the holy Doctor of the Church and mystic Bernard of Clairvaux in his call for the second crusade) or against the legality of torture (on the contrary, Pope Innocent IV introduced this evil and legitimized it). In those ecclesiastical documents we find edicts to persecute heretics and teachers of errors and to bring them to the stake, to compel under torture so called witches to confess their alliance with the devil, to have wives (officially concubines) of priests flogged or sold as slaves. The Church authorities and the grass-roots equally saw Jesus as the way to true life, they read and heard and meditated on how he stood up for people, they swore their oaths with a hand laid on his Gospel and they affirmed with the words of the first letter of John that God is love. And yet they behaved cruelly and heartlessly. All in the service of the God of love. Let anyone understand this who can.

In a Vatican document about early Church practice, Pope John-Paul II rightly recalled that our sense of historical relativity should not fail us, even with regard to our moral judgement of deeds, the pernicious character of which only later has become clear. For example, the Holy Inquisition's practice of torture. But these words of the Pope are little more than a sop to our consciences. The moral condemnation does not concern the people who were guilty of these acts, whether Pope or inquisitor or executioner or the roaring mob around the stake. The only question is: how could such practices, in a church which appeals to the gospel, not have evoked fierce protests? We have to wait until 1630 for the first clear protest against witch trials – more than a century after the beginning of this inhuman practice. In that year the book of the young Jesuit Friedrich von Spee von Langenfeld, *Cautio criminalis*, was published – anonymously because von Spee knew the threat of being arrested for defending the witches and being tortured until he confessed that he was himself an underling of the devil.

How could all of that happen? It was possible because people of that era belonged to a culture which still had a long way to go on the path of humanization. Only the cultural change which

came with the Enlightenment has opened our eyes to the horror
of traditional and uncritically followed customs. Human beings
can for a very long time remain blind to the disgusting nature of
what they do. Evolution is an extremely slow process. Only after
an immeasurably long period of growth and development is a
threshold reached, and only then can something truly new come
about. It can then often come about in a relatively short time.
And this is what happened in Western culture. Only with the
Enlightenment did it cross the crucial threshold. We can understand that. But no one can understand how it is possible that for
a thousand years even Christians were not at all worried by these
acts of inhumanity.

We, today's Christians, are heirs to the ethical ideas of the
past. We should not accept this inheritance without looking
critically at what is on the list. In drawing up this list we can be
aided by reference to the ethical views which we derive from the
axiom of modern faith and which are based on Jesus' message.
Even then the danger is still lurking that we steer clear of the
gospel. Human selfishness is not at all attracted by the gospel
and is incredibly subtle when it wants to neutralize it. But even if
we have left behind the classical teaching about original sin we
still have to realize that dark forces are at work in humanity
which resist further humanization. But this danger is considerably smaller in an ethics based on love than in a law-based
ethics. This should be clear from what follows.

Confrontation of the modern believer's ethics with pre-modern ethics

The error of pre-modern ethics is not that it formulates rules and
enacts laws. Every system of ethics must do that, otherwise it
remains an organism without a skeleton, a mollusk. A modern
believer's ethics will also need formulations and laws. The error
of pre-modern ethics lies in the fact that it absolutizes its laws.
And it cannot escape that error. Its laws come from God-in-
Heaven and are therefore on principle not subject to human
adaptations and corrections. This view must now and again
result in conflict with common sense, which teaches us that
sometimes allowances have to be made. Pre-modern ethics was
also aware of this and was always wise enough to make room for

such accommodations. Sometimes so much room that the same healthy common sense had to protest. Blaise Pascal's sharp criticism, in his *Lettres provinciales*, of the casuistry of which he accused contemporary Jesuits, was an expression of this protest. In fact, this casuistry reveals the contradiction inherent in pre-modern ethics, namely, that it confesses the sanctity and inviola-bility of the prescriptions distilled from the Bible while at the same time it sees the necessity, in practice, of cautiously circumventing them simply because it is impossible to observe them.

In most cases there will be no conflict between the laws of inner-worldly modern ethics and those coming from an outer world. In both systems the prescriptions equally reflect human experiences. Also those laws which are taken to be statements from God-in-Heaven are in fact the fruit of experience which teaches what is beneficial to life and living together and what is harmful. Appealing to the authority of God only secures these laws additional support. A modern believers' ethics looks to experience to find out what is necessary, if the humanizing impulse from God working deep within us is to be promoted or at least not hindered. Like the laws of pre-modern ethics, the modern ones also consist partly of prohibitions. They shut the door on behaviour that makes co-existence either impossible or very difficult. For example, theft, calumny, or perjury. And, of course, murder and terrorism, and causing chaos. Or discrimin-ation and racism. The laws also include commands. These formulate what as a rule is necessary for our own good and for the good of others. An example of this is the golden rule: treat others as you would wish them to treat you in the same circumstances; or to be reliable; or to keep promises; or to keep secrets that have been entrusted to you; or to look after your health; or to protect nature; or to beware of the modern addictions like pornography or alcohol and other intoxicants. These commands and prohibitions are binding because they teach us what as a rule promotes or harms the process of humanization.

For the most part the content of this ethics is identical with that of law-based ethics. But the accent lies elsewhere. In pre-modern ethics the observance of usually good laws is in the foreground, and in the background is God-in-Heaven, un-fortunately presented as an authority which gives commands and

prohibitions and which punishes and rewards. In the ethics of
the modern believer the inner call of fundamental Love at work
in us is in the foreground. In the background is the consideration
of how we can best put this call into practice. This in no way
contradicts heteronomous ethics, for instance, when it says that
abortion is wrong. For as a rule the impulse coming from God is
directed towards activity that promotes life. We arrive at the
crossroads when in a particular case the prohibition of abortion
will have dire consequences. In this case the two ethical systems
will part company. Pre-modern ethics will not ignore the
prohibition, since it comes from God and is therefore absolutely
binding. If a woman takes the risk of paying with her life for the
birth of the child rather than terminating the pregnancy, this
system of ethics will fully support her decision. Some time ago
the Vatican even beatified an Italian woman who brought her
child into the world at the cost of her own life. In this way the
Church authorities indicate that this is ideal behaviour. But at the
same time this ethics will approve of using all escape routes
which are not closed off by law in order to do what in these
circumstances seems reasonable. An example that was circu-
lating at that time and was never contradicted by a higher
authority and yet was not entirely substantiated was the
curettage of some nuns who were raped by black rebels in the
Belgian Congo in 1960. One did not know whether perhaps some
of them had become pregnant as a result of the rape. Perhaps one
did not want to know. For what was to be done in such a case?
Abortion was out of the question. That would be clearly acting
against God's commandment. On the other hand it was to be
avoided that nuns should gave birth to mulattos. But a so-called
curettage is not an abortion. It is a therapeutic procedure in the
interests of health. Thus what was seen as necessary and
responsible, was achieved without any talk of abortion. At least,
that is what was said.

The ethics of the modern believer will react differently in such
a case. All human acts are considered to have good and bad sides.
On the one hand they all have something which serves the
growth of love in people, but on the other hand there are
elements which harm this growth instead. This applies to abortion. In the modern believer's ethics the attempt will be made to
find where the greater good or the lesser evil lies, which is the
main point here. The law of God is helpful in this deliberation. It

formulates what, as a rule, promotes human development and what therefore has the best prospects of meeting the requirements of love. 'As a rule' means not always and everywhere. No single law is absolute, not even the divine law, precisely because it comes to us through a not totally reliable human medium. Only love is absolute. But what love demands is often anything but clear. And the danger of self-deception is always lurking – the danger that we do not choose the best thing but what is most attractive and easy. There is a kind of gravitational force within us, an unwillingness to allow ourselves to be lifted by love beyond the level we have achieved, for this often requires of us that we give up ourselves, something which we might want to avoid at all costs. Most abortions are carried out simply for selfish reasons, for example, not to endanger ascent on the career ladder, or following the motto 'no children, no burden'. Reflection on and pondering whether the driving force in making a decision is love or a justifiable concern for one's own good presupposes a skill which Ignatius Loyola, in a pre-modern expression, calls 'discernment of spirits'. In the *Spiritual Exercises* he gives direction on this. But often even this direction does not bring about certainty. In this case, one decision is as good as another, and there is no need to torture oneself with scruples after termination of a pregnancy.

If for good reasons one decides to break a law, one can always fall back on the already mentioned words of Paul to the Romans 13:8 that anyone who loves his neighbour, i.e. acts for his good, has complied with the whole of the Torah. Or other words of Paul, this time at the conclusion of chapter 12 of the first letter to the Corinthians, that the way that surpasses all other ways – even that of fidelity to the laws – is the way of love. Anyone who has been educated in a pre-modern spiritual climate and believes that he hears in the laws the unadulterated voice of God will at every step feel ill at ease at every step on forbidden territory and interpret this feeling as the nagging of his conscience. In reality, this nagging is only the reproving voice of the super-ego. This is the concept used by Sigmund Freud (1856-1938) to designate the commanding or forbidding voices of the educator, whose ethical guidelines one has interiorized since childhood. This super-ego resists the non-observance of its demands, because it is in danger of losing its power. But this loss of power is a blessing for man, for it is the beginning of his liberation. And Jesus saw it as his main mission to free mankind: in the language of tradition, to 'save' men – by letting them share in his own freedom.

CHAPTER FOUR

A Modern Believer's Sexual Ethics

An inner-worldly or modern believer's ethics will have to correct outer-worldly ethics in more than one domain. It will do this in any case with regard to its attitude towards property. In the past, pre-modern ethics virtually gave free rein to a liberal capitalism, the excesses of which are plaguing us today. Chapter Six will deal with this. A second area is the relationship to laws and customs bearing the positive name of obedience while in reality being an unevangelical submission to the established powers as required by the super-ego. Chapter Seven will deal with this. Finally, Chapter Eight will look in detail at the problem of euthanasia.

But a correction is required above all in sexual ethics. This problem will be dealt with in Chapter Four and Chapter Five. This is an area which reveals the horizontal schism between the pre-modern thinking of Church authorities and the modern thinking of the Church grassroots. 90% of Catholic married couples in the West use, without having a guilty conscience, contraceptive methods which were forbidden by the encyclical *Humanae Vitae*. And young couples who are believers do not hesitate to live together before marriage or are content to have a civil wedding, although that has always been branded by Rome as sinful concubinage. But this stigma likewise prevents only a few from remarrying after a divorce. All of this has become quite normal despite the unanimous teaching of Catholic moral theologians for hundreds of years about the sinfulness of every form of sexual pleasure outside of marriage and although pious literature, popular missions, catechism teaching and Sunday sermons have instilled this teaching so deeply in the psyche of believers that violations of the 6th and 9th commandments outweigh all other infringements. In less than half a century this thousand-year-old, seemingly indestructible edifice has collapsed like a house of cards. It is not by chance that this happened at the same time that modern thinking has, like a tsunami, completely flooded the dams which protected the spheres of life governed by the Church. It is quite obvious that the two phenomena are intrinsically connected. This link will be examined more closely in what follows.

What is the origin of our pre-modern sexual ethics?

First the hidden background to earlier sexual ethics should be brought to light. It has to do with a general rejection of all sexual pleasure within Christianity. Karen Armstrong notes in one of her works that of all the great religions Christianity is the only one which on principle distances itself from sexual pleasure. In all other religions the basic principle is: sexual pleasure? Yes, of course, except ... And then follow reservations, the fruit of experience that the sexual drive can also be destructive, so that in dealing with this drive safeguards are required. By contrast, the Christian motto is: sexual pleasure? No, of course, except that ... And then follows a series of conditions under which Church authorities consider sexual pleasure, by way of exception, to be no longer sinful, although they are also not openly said to be good. The conditions are: that the pleasure is experienced within a valid marriage; that the intention in intercourse is to beget a child; and that pleasure in this is not sought but accepted. The second condition was established under the influence of Augustine of Hippo, who was the most important theologian and author not only of the early fifth century but of the entire mediaeval Church. His ideas determined Church thinking for centuries. This second condition was then gradually weakened to the point where it was only required not to make begetting of a child impossible. This already limited freedom of sexual inter-course was, in the course of time, strictly narrowed down even further by Church authorities. It was necessary to abstain in Advent and during the forty days of Lent, on Ember Days and on vigils of great feasts, and also on the eve of a communion day. Pleasure, especially sexual pleasure, was clearly something very suspect. The Lord God did not like it. Carrying a burden was preferable to pleasure – at least physical pleasure, which is a cousin of lust, and lust conjures up a swamp of corruption. Thus it comes about that the concept 'immoral', which is basically a synonym for 'unethical', is now exclusively used for sexual behaviour which does not comply with the above-mentioned three conditions. The same applies to 'indecent' or 'licentious' or 'libertinage' or 'vice' and other similar words, as if morality was the same as abstinence. But corruption, abuse of power, slander and violence are much more unethical than running as a streaker across the tennis court at Wimbledon.

But spiritual pleasure was permissible. A few years ago, the catalogue of an exhibition of manuscripts and incunabula from old monastic libraries in Brabant bore as its title the words from a monastic librarian from that period: 'A sea of permissible pleasure'. In contrast to bodily pleasure spiritual pleasure was allowed. On the other hand we can wonder at the fact that Church tradition, despite its suspicion of physical pleasure, never condemned culinary and suchlike physical pleasures as sinful – a banquet with five courses, a bottle of old wine, bourbon, a comfortable room, a lounge chair, a Jacuzzi, a schnaps, ice cream, perfume, a siesta. Its response in these cases was 'yes, of course!', except when the need for such pleasures was over the top.

Only with regard to sexual pleasure, however slight it might be, was the opposite attitude, 'no, of course not!' But what is so different and so pernicious in this kind of pleasure that it should be considered mortally sinful? Surely not because it is physical? If so, the Church authorities would have to condemn all the above-mentioned unnecessary pleasures as well. And even the necessary ones, like sleeping, eating and drinking.

The further development of sexual ethics has consisted above all in a thorough examination of the whole sphere of sexual activity and in defining very exactly the degree of sinfulness of every detail. In all their utterances about these matters the moral theologians considered themselves to be spokesmen for the will of God. It is not by chance that these spokespersons were all men, so that sexual ethics had a one-sidedly male orientation. And almost without exception these male spokesmen were celibates who made judgements about things of which they could not have had the slightest knowledge based on experience.

With their ethical views they educated generations of young people. Strangely, the most obvious questions did not occur to their listeners or readers. For example, what is the foundation for all these prescriptions? Where in the Bible is the prohibition, accompanied by so many threats, against masturbation, pre-marital sex, French kissing, contraceptives? Or where does it say in the Bible that God forbids sexual pleasure and therefore makes it sinful and that under certain very definite conditions He turns a blind eye? And how can something which is sinful of itself, under these conditions suddenly be good or at least permitted? Is something which is good in itself not always and everywhere good? Or where does the sexual drive come from if not from God the creator, and how can a gift from God be bad in itself? Especially when the use of this gift is born of love? Human sexuality is distinguished from that of animals precisely through its capacity to express love and thereby to strengthen it. And why should precisely sexual pleasure be sinful and other pleasures of the kinds we saw above, which are just as physical, not be sinful?

These questions were simply not asked, because it was not possible, not permitted. They would have constituted a troublesome breach of taboo with very painful consequences for the questioner. The correct and liberating answer to these questions would naturally have been that these prohibitions were in no way based on divine directives, that they were the work of human beings, sometimes wise, often dubious, annoying, shameful. But the power of taboo made this answer unthinkable. The consequences were correspondingly bad: troubled conscience, anxiety, repression, complexes, psychic aberrations, or even the discredit incurred by the Church in modern society not least because of its sexual ethics; and finally, the avalanche it has thereby caused: the so-called sexual revolution of the 20th century in the Christian West, which has rushed ahead to opposite extremes which are just as ethically worrying and which have contributed just as little to true human development as has the earlier system of sexual ethics of the Roman Church.

Did the Church then, for lack of biblical arguments, have to have recourse to reason to produce arguments for condemning sexual pleasure? Of course, and it could do that. It could argue that the sexual drive is much stronger than other drives and exercises a much stronger attraction for people. It stifles much more easily the voice of reason and then sweeps away the freedom of decision. In this sense this drive represents a much greater danger to human values. The strength of this attraction can be measured by the immensity of the financial turnover of the modern sex industry. And just how much its power stands in the way of human development is seen from the crimes for which it is responsible: trafficking in women, prostitution, pornography, child abuse, rape.

An explanation of this phenomenon is to be found in the fact that sexual love in human evolutionary history emerged only late from the animal drive for reproduction and has by no means reached maturity. It is still only with plenty of effort that this drive lets itself be integrated into love. Often it manifests itself as a mere satisfaction of needs, turning, to the detriment of love, another person into a replaceable object, making this object subordinate to one's own desire, and in some cases even destroying it. With its reaction, 'sexual pleasure? No, of course!' the Church authorities have in mind the derailments which threaten when the sex drive no longer listens to the voice of reason. Just like nuclear energy, sexuality is a precious but dangerous force, difficult to harness and to be treated with caution. When integrated, it can be a marvellous enrichment to human life; out of control, it can wreak havoc and cause chaos. But for pure fear, the Church authorities have converted the necessary caution into rejection. They have thought they had to warn people ever anew against the sex drive, presenting it as a mortal danger. In this way they have not only omitted to promote the necessary integration of the sex drive and the controlling of chaos, but have even been a hindrance. In short, because of the danger of drowning they have forbidden swimming instruction. This has resulted in a continuous flow of drowning casualties .

But it is meaningless to deal with the real danger of enslavement through the use of fear complexes and prohibitive measures. To avoid lethal accidents on the motorways we should not limit driving on them except in very particular circumstances. The dangerous character of sexual pleasure is not a valid argument for condemning it. The argument is at most useful for cautioning people to exercise proper care. And this caution concerns not only those who, freely or otherwise, have committed themselves to celibacy. It is stupid to seek out what can excite in us the animal drive. In our society which abounds in sexual stimulation this calls for wise asceticism. The media offer us an abundance of occasions of voyeurism. Buddhist wisdom teaches that we should never ask: 'Is it allowed to do that?' To ask whether something is forbidden or not quite – after all, that is the meaning of the question – is to ask the wrong thing. To leave out something because it is forbidden (by whom, by the way?) awakens unconscious resistance against the ban and strengthens the tendency to do precisely what is forbidden. The phenomenon

of the attraction of forbidden fruit is familiar from time immemorial. And this unconscious resistance waits for its moment
and sooner or later seizes its opportunity. In Buddhist wisdom
the right question is: 'Do I accept all the consequences of my act?'
If after mature reflection a person finds the answer is yes, he
should do it; if the answer is no, he should not do it.

The sources of pre-modern sexual ethics

The danger arising from the sex drive is therefore no fundamental argument for mounting powerful prohibitions against
sexual pleasure as the Church authorities have done for centuries. Then there is the fact that for their commands and
prohibitions their last court of appeal was always the will of an
authority residing in an extramundane world. But precisely the
whole of the Old Testament, which the Church regards as the
word of the living God – as is loudly proclaimed every Sunday
after the reading – speaks a quite different language from that of
abstinence. From the very beginning it says that man is to
increase and multiply, which is precisely what cannot happen
through abstaining. Again, the Bible treats eroticism and sexual
intercourse as the most normal thing in the world, and in the so-
called Song of Solomon it is celebrated even in lyrical tones, even
though differently from those of the Kama Sutra. In Israel as well
the motto was 'sexual pleasure, yes, of course, except ...'. Clearly
this did not stop the Christian tradition from reversing things.
Very early on there must have been factors very different from
the word of God determining the Church's negative attitude. The
rejection of sexual pleasure is indeed the result of the convergence of a whole series of views, historical influences,
traditions and sensitivities, which created a complex network in
which the various factors reinforced one another. Through the
process of tradition the rejection was handed down uncritically
from one generation to the next and in this way has left its mark
on the whole development. It is easy to rip apart a few hemp
fibres, but not once they are woven with a lot of other fibres into
a rope. Something similar applies to the web of views about
sexuality within the Church. In his book *The Body and Society:
Men, Women, and Sexual Renunciation in Early Christianity
from 50 to 450* (1988) the American theologian Peter Brown has

expertly indicated the many elements comprising this web. Here we can only offer a rudimentary sketch of them.

The point of departure of that evolution was the almost exclusive preoccupation of the early Church with the Ultimate, the Kingdom of God, as Jesus called it. To that extent the Church was right, and even today Christians should share that concern, which is of a different and higher order than the everyday concerns – to which sexuality also belongs. This limited its importance from the very beginning, but the limitation developed gradually into disdain and then rejection. There were many different elements involved in this process: the Church's conviction that the end was nigh and that therefore there was not much sense in marrying and begetting children; the need for self-control and external dignity which did not permit the civilized Roman man to give free rein to lust; the view of the very influential Origin in the 3rd century that sexual intercourse supported the cycle of birth and death, whereas Jesus had come precisely to conquer death and give immortality; the rejection of marriage (and enjoyment of wine), on the basis of mythical/-mystical views, by the rigorist Tatian (c. 170) and his followers; the experience of the hermits in the Egyptian desert in the 4th and 5th centuries that the rejection of all sexual activity opened a way to inner peace and deeper contemplation; the influential teaching of Manichaeism, which even ensnared Augustine, that the body, and especially sexuality was the sphere of influence of the evil divinity and that man had to seek at all costs liberation from this sphere; for many young girls the rejection of a future as a productive womb in the service of an often brutal husband assigned to them, and therefore the choice of the unmarried state, which then step by step became a religious state under the name of virginity consecrated to God; the almost morbid glorification of this virginity in the 4th century by the eloquent Bishop Ambrose of Milan, who was listened to with great reverence. Probably the most important role in this anti-sexual development was played by Augustine. He had keenly observed and analysed the disorder within man and accounted for it as a result of the sin of Adam and Eve, which used to be regarded as historical fact. Thus he came to the idea of original sin, which he saw as handed on by the sex drive, for precisely this drive led to the procreation of children and therefore to the handing on of original sin. And this original sin was no laughing matter, for if it was not taken away by baptism eternal damnation was unavoidable.

These many and still further elements combined to form an invincible rejection of sexual activity, resulting in the attitude referred to above: 'Sexual pleasure? Of course not! Except ...'. Perhaps an important element in this disappointing result is the fact that nowhere in all of these considerations is there any mention that sexual intercourse could be an expression of tenderness and a reinforcement of mutual love, and thus a sign of a deeply human encounter. As if sexuality could be understood merely as the expression of animal desire and as unfortunately the only way to beget offspring.

The damaging effects of the Church's sexual psychosis have often been attacked, but usually there has been no mention of its effects on women, although the downgrading of women is just as bad a product of this psychosis. The hierarchies, theologians, moral theologians, monks, parish priests, preachers, all celibate men with repressed sexual needs, felt a sexual attraction to many a reasonably good-looking woman and experienced it as an ongoing invitation to sin. They set up defences against this. Also with the pen. The things that flowed from their pens about the deception, the harm, the badness, the loathsomeness, the dangers associated with women are more than shameful. Obviously, they were trying in this way to write themselves free of their sexual obsessions. The fact that today in Rome, despite all the fine-sounding statements, there is still a refusal to acknowledge woman's complete equality with man is rooted in this worrying past.

Birth of a new sexual ethics

For the binding force of its prohibitions and for the seriousness of the eternal punishments involved, the Church authorities, without further justification, appealed to God-in-Heaven. The transition to an autonomous view of the world causes a complete collapse of all its teaching about sexuality and requires a completely new approach. This renewal, incidentally, has already been happening for some time. Its influence is being felt even in Rome, in the central bastion of tradition-bound thinking. There, in the past, the primary aim of sexual intercourse was always taken to be the begetting of children, and a modest second aim was the calming of sexual impulses, according to the words of Paul, who writes in 1 Corinthians 7:9 that it is better to marry than to 'burn' – with desire. But in the 20th century the central authorities of the Church have suddenly discovered that marriage can also have as its meaning and aim the mutual enrichment of the couple.

What at is the source of this enlightenment? It comes not from above but from below, from the grassroots believers, who became ever more sensitive to the value of modern ideas even with regard to sexuality. They liberated themselves from traditional thinking and from the accompanying fears and took no further notice of Rome's prohibition of the use of contraceptives, of pre-marital sex, of remarriage after divorce. For the time being it is still unthinkable that Rome will listen to the grassroots also with regard to these prohibitions. The encyclical *Humanae Vitae* presents too massive a barrier. But with the admission that marriage and hence sexual intercourse is for the mutual enrichment of the couple, the Church authorities have, under pressure from the grassroots, ventured to take a step forward. This justifies the assumption that grassroots pressure will bring about further adjustments. This is also absolutely necessary, not only because the rift between the Church leadership and the grassroots is a disaster, but also and above all because heaven, to which the Church leadership appeals to justify its directives, has become for modern people a mythological construct without any real meaning. Thus the whole ethics of sexuality, which Church tradition had suspended from this heavenly vault, came crashing down in the 1960s with a loud bang. The very restrictive moral teaching of the past has had to make way for the so-called sexual liberation, i.e. sex as satisfying a need. The result was the impregnation of advertising with sexual themes, the love parades, the sex shops and peepshows, the acceptability of magazines like 'Playboy', the pornographic websites on the internet, which have up to fifty million clicks per day. This flood is no cause for surprise. For centuries the Church made of sexual pleasure a desirable fruit which, however, was forbidden by God, with eternal punishments threatened for those who dared to partake of it. But it could not show the reasonableness of this prohibition. With the death of this prohibiting God the fear of enjoying large helpings of the long desired fruit disappeared also. No wonder we are today confronted with ruins.

The complete collapse of the earlier ethics of sexuality at least has the advantage that space became available for a new, now inner-worldly and at the same time genuinely Christian ethics. Its foundation is the insight that our mission as human beings consists in growing in love. Precisely in this way eroticism, more than any other feelings of pleasure, promotes our human development. It is a way of human encounter and union in tenderness and care. But there is also the necessity to silence the warning voice of the super-ego which calls this pleasure 'sinful'. Even when we find that we have succeeded in this, for a long time we still hear the receding echo of this voice. The centuries-long views instilled in us have bitten too deep not to have left some scars. And yet it is true that between sexual pleasure and other forms of enjoyment there is no essential distinction, but only one of degree. Sexual pleasure is simply much more intense and precisely for this reason much more threatening. It leads much more easily to loss of freedom and to addiction. The temptation to settle for a level of life that is impoverished because not altruistic is therefore much greater. If sexual experience is not to remain a form of infantile regression it needs a thorough-going purification. This is not a question of strength of will but of mindfulness, respect and tenderness.

Fundamentals of a modern Christian ethics of sexuality

What does an ethics of sexuality which proceeds directly from the principles of a modern believer's vision look like? While in the Church's former textbooks on morality that ethics took up page after page, the intra-mundane ethics of sexuality needs much less space. It is based on the idea that sexual pleasures are good to the extent that they are expressions of love (which covers a broad spectrum: from very little to very much). Love means here something different from being in love. Being in love includes much that is love, but it is still mixed with need and desire. Both of these are precisely not love because their aim is the self, whereas love goes out from the self and encounters the other person.

The transition from law-based ethics to ethics based on love will have tangible consequences, especially where law and its condemnations cannot stand up to the believer's reason or where they do not take the crucial role of love into account. An example of the first kind is the spectre that used to be made of masturbation. This spectre is not the product of the last century, as is often thought. Its history can be traced back into the era of the fathers of the Church. It does not originate from the Bible, which simply does not mention it. The text of Genesis 38:9 which for want of a better one used to be cited earlier and which explained the name 'onanism' is not concerned with masturbation but with *coitus interruptus*. Yahweh does punish Onan, but only because he fails in his social obligation. His duty was to have a child with Tamar, the widow of his deceased brother, whom according to levirate law he had to marry, and the child was then to be considered the child of his brother and not his. And this he does not want.

How does the Church justify, without a biblical foundation, its strict condemnation of masturbation? With a two-fold argument. It is to be found in no. 2352 of the *Catechism of the Catholic Church*. The first says: the Church authorities have unanimously condemned masturbation from time immemorial. But this only repeats the condemnation without giving proper reasons. The second argument is that the faithful have always felt it to be wrong. Yet there is no doubt that this feeling is due to the constant condemnation by the Church authorities. And so this second argument is also very wobbly. Does that mean that nothing can be said ethically against masturbation? That is not true either. The ethical quality of sexual actions is determined by the love encounter they express. In masturbation precisely this encounter is missing. It fixates a person on the self, and such a fixation is characteristic of someone who has not yet reached maturity. But the fact that an adolescent goes through a stage of masturbation gives us no grounds for complaint. It is only bad if he gets stuck there. Being truly human requires that we reach maturity also in the sexual sphere. This maturity is achieved through the encounter in love. It is regrettable that in masturbation this is missing, but that does not in any way justify the threats of mortal sin and hell which used to be associated with it. Besides, the concept sin belongs to pre-modern modes of expression. Love speaks a different language.

An example of the second kind in which the decisive role of love is not taken into account is the blanket condemnation of homophilia. For this condemnation the above-mentioned catechism can this time, in no. 2357, without any problem appeal to the Bible. The Torah demands the death penalty for such dreadful behaviour, a sign that Yahweh abhors it and that therefore it must be a mortal sin. It is true that in the whole Torah there are only two verses (Lev. 18:22 and 20:13) which condemn homosexual intercourse, and these are lost in the multitude of other sexual prescriptions. But Paul also considers homophilia to be perverse, and in his letter to the Romans he fulminates against it without inhibition. That was obviously enough for the whole Church tradition, down to the present, to condemn it. But here a couple of not insignificant things were overlooked. First, that for Israel's survival it was necessary to set itself clearly apart from neighbouring peoples and their religious and ethical views and practices. But these neighbours tolerated and practised homosexuality. Only by means of such lines of demarcation was Israel able to maintain its own identity, so that in the melting pot of the races and cultures of the Middle East it did not go under and disappear. Second, that in the Torah the condemnation of homophilia was only one of the many expressions of its almost obsessive concern for cultic purity. We only need to read Leviticus 11-15, where there are four whole chapters of such prescriptions concerning cleanliness, which fundamentally express fear and anxiety. In the eyes of the Jews, access to Yahweh – a condition of possibility of salvation – depended on such purity. But we no longer belong to the Jewish people with their religious obsession with purity, and we have no need, as a Church, to shut ourselves off in order to survive. But it is still more important that statements in the Bible and in tradition only have validity for modern believers if they do not contradict reason. For the *Catechism*, however, the biblical statements are enough to justify a blanket condemnation of homophilia. Still, no. 2357 attempts to support this condemnation with an argument from reason, namely that sexual activity, by its very nature, is geared towards procreation. If this is impossible from the outset, as in homosexual relationships, intercourse contradicts the law inscribed in nature by God. Homosexual activity is therefore in contradiction to God's will and is therefore sinful and morally reprehensible. But to be logical, the Catechism would have to say the same for sexual intercourse after the menopause and during pregnancy, which it wisely does not do. Ethics based on love like that of the modern believer has a different starting point. It asks about the degree of love in a relationship. And the Bible does not ask about that. Whether a homosexual relationship is union of love or not is of no importance for the Bible. The fact that in Leviticus 18:22-23 and again in 20:13 and 15-16 homosexuality is mentioned in the same breath with bestiality shows clearly that the Bible is not thinking of a loving encounter between persons. Thus it is not possible to use the Bible in arguing for the condemnation of a homosexual relationship when it is born of a love which is just as firm as that in a heterosexual relationship.

Agreements and differences

In other respects the concrete prescriptions of pre-modern sexual ethics and the ethics of the modern believer largely coincide. Both reject adultery, polygamy, prostitution, paedophilia, bestiality. But the basic views are different. Pre-modern ethics justifies its prohibitions with the help of law, whether biblical law or the God-given natural law, so that infringements call for punishment by the divine law-giver. The ethics of the modern believer justifies them from the need, intrinsic to our inner being, for human encounter and union, a need which is the fingerprint of the divine essence in us. Not responding to this need alienates us from our own foundation, which is the fundamental divine Love, and results in pitiful impoverishment.

The way adultery is judged is a practical example of the difference in approach. Adultery is basically a form of polygamy. In heteronomous ethics it is a serious breach of the divine command supported by Jesus. That is enough and usually no one asks for what reason the good Lord God cannot possibly agree to it. But if one does ask the question the answer is usually sought in the exclusive right, given in marriage, that each partner has to the body of the other. And the good Lord God sees to it that this right is protected. He cannot do otherwise, because He is supreme justice. But then how can Yahweh in the Torah not merely tolerate polygamy, as with Abraham, Jacob or Moses, but even actively promote it, as with King David? Do we not read in 2

Samuel, 12:8 that Yahweh, when Saul is slain, gives to David all of Saul's women or, as the Bible says so graphically, gave them into his lap? Besides, the reference to the 'exclusive right to the body of the partner' is nonsense. It would mean degrading a human relationship to a relationship between owner and possession. In antiquity the master had an exclusive right to the body of his slaves, male or female. They were his property, things he possessed. He could do what he liked with this possession – whip his slave or sexually abuse his female slave. Is a man allowed to do what he likes to his wife? Does he have the right to beat her when he is enraged against her? Perhaps he is allowed to do that in Islam, but no longer in a culture in which man and woman are seen as equal. Adultery has nothing to do with a breach of property rights, even if the Torah sees it like that. A person is never a possession. But adultery is an offence against the exclusive intimacy of the couple, and in a monogamous society this is at the heart of the love relationship. Anyone who starts having an affair shows in fact that his or her intimacy with the partner was not genuine or at least not exclusive. The partner was exchangeable. Love cannot accept this. Instead of law the norm for sexual ethics is love and the human development which it promotes.

On the other hand, the law teaches us what normally promotes human development and therefore what is compatible with love. In general its requirements are sound, which leads us to the question of how the modern believer's ethics judges certain kinds of behaviour which are condemned by the Bible and tradition, i.e. by the wisdom of law, but which are quite common in modern society.

First, divorce. In fact, tradition condemns not so much divorce as remarriage of divorced persons. In this the Church is not acting according to the mind of Jesus. In Mark 10:9 he condemns divorce as such, since it is contrary to the will of God. Here there is no mention of remarriage. This is only mentioned in verse 11. The Church authorities see it differently. For the kind of factual divorce, which in the Catechism no. 1650 is called 'separation from bed and board', they show understanding, and they have no problem with a civil divorce of baptized persons (because they regard the vows in a civil marriage as null and void). They should even be glad if the couple shakes the civil dust from their baptized feet. However, even civil divorce is the confirmation, much regretted by Jesus, that God's plan has been thwarted. But whereas the Church authorities will under no circumstance tolerate remarriage, the factual consensus is growing in the Church that this stubborn attitude in Rome is wrong. Can the view of the grassroots faithful be justified as legitimate? The answer is rather complicated. It needs to be dealt with in a separate chapter – Chapter Five, which follows.

Another clear distinction between Roman law-based ethics and the beliefs of Christian modernity concerns pre-marital sexual intercourse, understood as co-habitation of an unmarried couple. This does not at all refer to merely superficial amorous escapades after chance meetings, which are part of the phenomena of decadence in a consumer oriented society. On the contrary, included in the term 'pre-marital' is the couple's intention of later entering into an official marriage or at least becoming a permanent couple although without any official declaration in church or before a civil authority, as was the case of a 'secret marriage' until the Council of Trent forbade it. A few centuries later this practice, in the past loaded with mortal sin and still a grave annoyance for the older generation, is the most normal thing in the (Western) world. From a believer's point of view there is not really much to be said against it. To quote the Bible's condemnation of fornication is useless. First it would be necessary to show that the concept 'fornication' is applicable here. Fornication is essentially sexual intercourse without commitment. It listens only to one's own desires and is out after instantaneous sexual gratification without a true encounter with the partner. The contemptuous word 'fornication' is out of place where there is a genuine attachment in love between two people. A genuine bond in love includes continuity, the will to be true to one another even without an official commitment in front of witnesses. It does not keep any back door open. And here also the principle applies that everything done out of love is good to that extent.

What, then, is the value or use of the official commitment before witnesses? It confirms in the social sphere what has previously only been a personal commitment, and thereby reinforces it. The Church and/or civil society represented by the witnesses consciously or otherwise exert pressure on the couple to stay together. This does not amount to an intrusion on their privacy. Each person is essentially a social being. As a monad he is no less a cell belonging to a totality. If family or friends regularly see someone with a woman other than his wife, they will be frowning in disapproval and he will feel that his behaviour is considered wrong. This moral disapproval is a form of 'lateral pressure' which will not be put on a couple whose relationship is still only developing. This couple does not have to stay together at all costs. To refuse such help from society betrays, along with an overestimation of one's own capabilities, an unconscious lack of concern for the good of one's partner, who wholeheartedly hopes for the marriage to succeed. And the duty of 'becoming one flesh', as the title of the next chapter will be called, drawing on words from the Book of Genesis, is not all that simple. These words from the Bible were earlier wrongly understood to mean sexual intercourse, whereas much more is involved. They refer to the existential unity, and this goes very deep and is lasting. To achieve it, requires time and effort, and help should always be welcome.

And what about contraception? Here, too, there is a yawning chasm between Rome's prescriptions and actual modern practice, even in the case of modern believers. But the distinction between prescription and practice is not directly concerned with sexual behaviour. Even prudish Rome acknowledges the acceptability of birth control. The distinction refers to the means. According to the teaching of the encyclical *Humanae Vitae*, which has never been withdrawn, it is not permissible to assist nature a little by chemical or mechanical means. To achieve its goal it has, in its wisdom, come up with its own solution: periodic abstinence. One should, with reverence, let nature have its way, for to intervene in this wonderful process on one's own authority is to interfere with the handiwork of the good Lord God. But the picture changes immediately when it is a question of restoring health. Nature, in its wisdom, has discovered a solution when bacteria attack the organism. Crowds of white blood corpuscles attack the invaders in order to eliminate them. But everyone, even in the Vatican, finds that it is no interference in the work of the Lord God, if one comes to the aid of nature's defences by using antibiotics. Experience has taught even the Vatican that nature's defences are often insufficient for achieving the goal. Likewise, experience has taught – but not in the Vatican – that the natural method of birth control often does not succeed in keeping the number of children to the desired limit. What is good in one case, can hardly be bad in the other. If one argues that the aim in the use of antibiotics is good but not in the use of contraceptives, the discussion is then switching from the means to the aim. It is no longer dealing with the means. It can often be the case that for egotistical reasons people do not follow Rome's directives, that, in the spirit of consumer society people want to shut themselves up in an existence that is neither blessed with children nor burdened with them. But at this point we are far removed from sexuality and moral judgements about it.

Finally, the modern believer's approach is not without consequences for *celibacy*. The choice for the celibate state sprang from the conviction that a life without sexual fulfilment was especially pleasing to God-in-Heaven. Today this choice can only be justified if it becomes clear that by giving up this fulfilment there is more human gain than loss. There is no doubt that human loss is involved. A whole sphere of human enrichment remains closed off to the celibate person. But the facts show that the gain can richly compensate for the loss. In its contemplative form celibacy can lead to great inner freedom and human fulfilment, which is seen not only in the lives of Christian but also Buddhist monks. But celibacy can also be meaningful in an active form where a person is so fully committed to working for the good of his fellow men that there is hardly any room left for an enduring union with a sexual partner and for rearing the children who would normally be born from this union. In an explicitly Christian form this celibacy can be a condition for committing oneself exclusively to that renewed world which Jesus called the 'Kingdom of God'. In each of these two forms, the contemplative and the active, celibacy can be justified.

But the Church authorities think that there is a third justification for celibacy: the priesthood. But this view does not stand up to the scrutiny of the modern believer. It is based on a two-fold pre-modern presupposition. First, that the priest in Christianity, as in pre-Christian religions, is the man who – on authority from the supernatural sacred world – has been allotted the task of functioning as a mediator between it and our profane world. However, his real task is to be a leader giving direction to the community of believers in matters of faith. The second presupposition is that sexual intercourse brings with it at least cultic impurity, whereas only the 'pure' are worthy to approach that supernatural world. The first presupposition, of course, loses all foundation if with modernity we have relinquished the division of reality into two worlds. The second supposition is a conviction for which Leviticus offers defence and which the Church cherished from early times, either consciously or unconsciously, but which this chapter has fundamentally put paid to.

Chapter Five

Indissoluble?

The content of this chapter was originally a part of the previous one. But this section grew so excessively that it was finally bursting at the seams and became a chapter in its own right. Why deal so much in detail with the indissolubility of marriage? Because the views of the grassroots and those of the Church authorities are so far apart. Who is right, and who is wrong? Or does the truth lie somewhere in the middle? In areas of dense population in the West the number of divorces is reaching the 50% mark. The Christian community is right in not finding this acceptable. Added to this, divorce often means remarriage, and in this the couple are in direct collision with an age-old Church tradition which strictly forbids remarriage after divorce and does not acknowledge it as marriage but condemns it as concubinage. Thus such couples are considered and treated as public sinners and are pushed to the outer margin of the Church. Only those who themselves have not known sexual intimacy, as one presupposes is true of the Church leadership, can see it as normal and even as required that the separated parties should spend the rest of their lives without this intimacy. While the Church in the West is already continually losing huge numbers of its members, it sees itself, out of fidelity to certain biblical texts and old customs, unfortunately forced to exclude an ever-increasing number of its remaining members. Earlier it used to be just exceptional cases, but today we are talking about thousands upon thousands. This exclusion consists in a kind of excommunication whereby the Church authorities refuse these public sinners communion. A new love relationship must in their eyes be much worse than corruption or political dishonesty or the behaviour of a Pinochet, to whom communion was never refused. At the same time they find that it belongs to their pastoral duty to preoccupy themselves with the fate of these members they have marginalized. Thus the theme of pastoral care for those who have married again after divorce, occurs again and again in their documents. They see them as lost sheep, people who live in sin. The bishops search for strategies to make the fate of these victims of the law more bearable, but they avoid making any changes to Church law. Yet they also want to avoid falling out with anyone. Another sign of their concern for the good of the victims of indissolubility, without doing any harm to this indissolubility, is their readiness to see whether what seemed to be a marriage was not – without people realizing it – in fact concubinage, which then not only could but indeed should be dissolved. They do this at the request of the marriage partners who want to escape from their marriage, usually to enter a new and hopefully better relationship. Thus they start to dig around in the couple's past in the hope of finding indications of the invalidity of a marriage which outwardly seemed valid. But these are, as will soon become clear, big steps on the wrong path.

The Torah on divorce and adultery

The Church teaching that the marriage bond is indissoluble and that a violation of this is sinful is deeply rooted in tradition. But in this case tradition is merely continuing biblical notions. For this reason it is essential that the basic biblical material be investigated carefully and critically. Perhaps the result will be that Church teaching about divorce and the punishment that goes with it is very much open to challenge. So, what do we learn from an examination of the Bible texts which form the basis of the Church's provisions and prohibitions?

With a clear conscience we can put aside texts from the Old Testament, since, insofar as the New Testament has not adopted them, they have no further relevance to us. Some views found in the Torah are today even reprehensible. Above all, that in marriage a woman is the possession of her husband rather than an equal partner. This possession is infinitely valuable to him because it allows him to live on in the progeny which the woman is to bring into the world for him. An extramarital relationship of the wife is a serious infringement of the proprietary right of the husband. The Torah punishes such a crime with death – and indeed by stoning. Because of the asymmetrical relationship between husband and wife the same condemnation and punishment do not apply to the husband. Sexual intercourse between him and a prostitute or a slave or an unmarried woman does not count as adultery. And, by the way, this means that in contrast to the Church the Torah does not view sexual intercourse as sinful in itself but at the most as a cause of cultic impurity. It also considers polygamy to be completely legitimate, for since the marriage bond is essentially one of ownership, the man can own several wives, just as he can own several plots of land or several houses or cows. Thus in 1 Kings 11:3 there is absolutely no objection to King Solomon's having 700 wives and 300 concubines. It is only held against him that those 700 wives were foreign princesses who misled him into the worship of other gods.

At that time it was possible for the husband to end the marriage unilaterally simply by issuing a document announcing a divorce and rejecting his wife. A wife could not do the equivalent. In a modern culture in which the woman is in principle equal to the man such morality favouring the husband cannot be the norm. We can therefore leave aside the Old Testament notion of morality regarding marriage, except where in a revised form it lives on in the New Testament.

What is the teaching of the New Testament?

Matthew 5:28 reinforces, with even greater severity, the Old Testament prohibition of adultery contained in the Ten Commandments: to look with lust at a (married!) woman already amounts to adultery. This view is already anticipated to some extent in the 9th commandment in Exodus 20:17. Because Jesus continues the views of the Torah, one must logically conclude that without committing adultery it is still possible to desire an unmarried woman, for in this case no sexual ownership right is violated. On the other hand, in open contradiction to Deuteronomy 24:1 Jesus explains that it does not matter whether a man rejects his wife with or without a document announcing divorce. The marriage remains a marriage in any case. To this extent Jesus rejects the Jewish moral teaching favouring men. But in order to survive, at that time a woman needed a man. The financial situation of a widow (a rejected woman was in fact a grass widow) was extremely precarious, and for this reason she had to find a new husband. But this made her, according to Matthew 5:32, an adulteress and her new husband an adulterer. The reason is that the rejected woman was still married to her first husband. But with this thesis Jesus (or Matthew?) is in head-on collision with modernity. Could it be that that this biblical thesis is only valid as long as one lives in the intellectual world of the Torah? Jesus belonged to Jewish culture and in some things affirmed the ideas of this culture although it was a product of its time, and even where this culture – without his being aware of it – contradicted his own basic intuition. The following pages will deal with this more in detail.

By the addition of the 'fornication clause' the stark reinforcement of the Torah is corrected in Matthew 5:32 and 19:9. Although marriage is indissoluble and remarriage after divorce (or rejection) is adultery, this is no longer the case if the grounds for divorce (or rejection) were *porneia*, which is usually translated as fornication. What exactly is meant by this is not explained further. Very probably it is a case of adultery on the part of the woman, for in the Torah the husband was allowed to take some liberties, at least with an unmarried woman. In any case, the clause implies that also in the New Testament marriage can definitely be finished in certain circumstances. This finding, however, destroys the theory of the essential indissolubility of marriage on which the whole of Church practice regarding marriage is based. For if indissolubility belongs to the very essence of marriage it can never cease to be part of it. Even fornication clauses cannot change anything. But if it is not an essential part of marriage it is simply a legal stipulation, and like every legal stipulation it is subject to a human authority. More about this later.

First, a word about the only text in the whole Bible from which one could conclude that the wife, too, could put her husband away, namely, Mark 10:12. Neither Matthew nor Luke included this verse. 'Put away' can only mean 'leave', since she had no power over her husband, whereas he did over her. Therefore she can leave him, but even then, says Jesus, she remains bound to him. If she marries again, she is committing adultery. This is also Paul's view in 1 Corinthians 7:10-11: she is allowed to leave her husband, but is not allowed to remarry. For Paul too marriage is indissoluble. But then he speaks more in detail about the problem of mixed marriages. If a Christian girl marries a heathen partner who wants a divorce, the woman does not need to consider herself as bound to him any longer. She is free and can marry again. In the secret language of the Church this right is called the Pauline Privilege (*privilegium Paulinum*). This privilege has never been questioned by the Church authorities. But here the same problem arises as with the fornication clause referred to above. If indissolubility is of the essence of marriage, as the Church teaches, how can a mixed marriage be dissolved? Does Paul perhaps have the right to change the essence of marriage? Of course not. Instead, it seems that his healthy human understanding has here triumphed over abstract theory.

If the Bible is no longer read as a book originating from an infallible other world but, as modern believers see it, as a book written by inspired human beings, naturally it loses the binding force given to every one of its statements. The texts quoted above simply formulate the convictions of the Jewish people at a particular phase of their cultural history, the convictions of Jesus who was a child of that people, and the convictions of Paul of Tarsus who was a scribe belonging to that race. These convictions can indeed be very valuable, but we are not obliged to obey them, even if there is a biblical aura surrounding them. The only thing that can command our obedience is the truth. What the Bible says about marriage has therefore only its own value, and we are to judge about that for ourselves, following reason and our hearts.

Wheat and chaff in the biblical moral teaching about marriage

The Torah, and the New Testament insofar as it follows the Torah, and the Church insofar as it loyally follows both of these, are right when they oppose divorce. It is a disaster. A promising beginning ends in a fiasco. The love which human beings aspire to does not come to fruition and thereby the couple lose both the richness of human development and the joys which grow out of it. Besides, as a rule it is a catastrophe for the children. And so every possible avenue should be explored to prevent it. The prohibition in the Torah and in Church tradition is the expression of an often helpless concern. Precisely because of this concern the Church refuses to accept the dissolution of a marriage. Once married, always married, until death separates the couple. Anyone who nevertheless still dares to marry again is a public sinner in the eyes of the Church and is threatened with eternal punishment in the other world. By these means the Church tries to prevent the break-up of marriages. Even civil society attempts this by requiring a judge's verdict, by offering advantages to married people, and also by imposing financial obligations on the financially stronger party, which formerly was always the man.

Rights and obligations of married people one-sidedly reflect the view of males. This one-sidedness harbours a whole host of injustices, and this to a large extent disqualifies the Torah's notions about marriage. Insofar as the New Testament and tradition distil their demands and prohibitions from the Old Testament we should reject them. They are Jewish notions born of a male and therefore unjust view of marriage. In no way do we need to attribute any eternal value to them.

But with regard to the New Testament, which speaks of Jesus' own notions, the situation is different. Christians find it quite natural to listen to the words of Jesus even when they contradict our own spontaneous tendencies and opinions. On the other hand we cannot see him as almighty and omniscient. We should recognize human limitations in him. He was a Jew living in a particular age and it could be that particular statements of his are no longer acceptable to modern believers. For this reason we will need to look critically at his words about marriage.

We have two kinds of statements by Jesus. The first consists of those in which he is simply repeating the prescriptions of the Torah, as one would expect of a Rabbi. The second kind consists of those in which he clearly strikes out on a path of his own. The first kind includes the condemnation of adultery and even of adulterous desires, in line with his words in Matthew 15:19, where he looks on the human heart as the root of all evil. Matthew 19:4-6 belongs to the second kind where he expresses his own deep intuition. Here he uses Genesis 2:24. In this text the Old Testament author interprets the mating drive as the drive towards a fundamental union. In this interpretation Jesus sees his own interpretation. He, too, sees marriage in this light. But at the same time he constructs from it his decisive argument for the legal indissolubility of marriage. Wrongly, as will now become clear. First a careful analysis of the Genesis text will be necessary and then of the way Jesus handles it.

Jesus on marriage and divorce in his interpretation of Genesis 2:24

Genesis 2:24 continues on from the forming of Eve from one of Adam's ribs and continues with the well-known text: 'Therefore man leaves father and mother and cleaves to his wife and they become one flesh.' But this text is not yet about marriage but about forming a bond, attaching one's heart, and therefore forming a couple. Marriage is only a juridical complement, a social construct which as such is relative to a particular culture. That it is relative in this way is indicated by the Jewish notion of marriage described above, according to which the woman is seen as part of the man's possessions. In modernity, this notion has served its time.

For the biblical author, what follows from this 'bond' equals 'becoming one flesh'. With the image 'one flesh' he expresses very succinctly how deep a personal union will be achieved by the forming of a couple, because 'flesh' in Semitic thinking refers to the whole person – body and soul. With 'become' there is the indication that the forming of the couple does not automatically bring about the profound union. This remains an ideal, the mature fruit of a long process of growth. It contains a call to make the mutual bond (mutual, although Genesis only speaks of the man as binding himself) so strong that it cannot be broken. Only then are man and wife 'one flesh'. This unity is existential and transcends the juridical level of indissolubility by far. How does one know that it has come about? When the two are separated by circumstances and have no rest until they are together again. By comparison with the existential union expressed in the image 'become one flesh' the legal unit with which Church marriage law is concerned is only secondary, almost a pure fiction. When a marriage entered into in accordance with all the prescriptions is separated from the existential union and yet is still considered to have juridical weight and the capacity to survive – thanks to external lateral pressure – it is in today's cultural climate guaranteed to collapse for lack of an internal binding force.

What does Jesus do with this Genesis text? First, he presents the whole process of the couple's developing into a union as a divine initiative. With this in view, at the end he adds a few words which are unobtrusive but crucial for his argument: 'What

God has put together.' This clause is not in the Genesis text. There nothing is 'put together'. There we only read that the husband binds himself to his wife. From the point of view of the modern believer this addition by Jesus can be accepted if one sees in the force that drives the two to union a self-revelation of fundamental love. But this was not Jesus' mind-set. He was probably thinking of the juridical indissolubility, the validity of which received support from his slight adjustment of the Genesis text.

A second slight adjustment is found in the tone. The tone in Genesis 2:24 is one of observation: a man leaves his parents to cleave to his wife, and the two become one flesh. But Jesus links this step, by using an explanatory 'therefore', with the preceding sentence: 'as man and woman God created them', which, however, is taken from a different context, namely Genesis 1:27. Yet in 2:24 the reason why the man cleaves to the woman is that she is bone from his bone and flesh from his flesh. The reason, therefore, is their original unity which wants to be restored. But if the man cleaves to the woman because God in creating them has made them complementary, the union of the couple is no longer merely an observable fact but the plan and will of God. In the same vein Jesus makes of the observational present tense a future tense resembling an imperative: 'Therefore *will* the man ... and she *become* ...' The imperative character of this manner of speaking is suggested with the help of a second addition to the original Genesis text: '... and that God said'. This text also is not in the Genesis text. Thus Jesus is making the observational words of the author into divine commands, which is meant to give them a much greater authority and binding force. Finally, he changes 'becoming one flesh' into 'being one flesh'. Thus he gives the impression that the bond represents an already accomplished union. That, too, is meant to give plausibility to the essential indissolubility of marriage.

The thing that is most open to criticism, however, is the juridical conclusion for which he has paved the way in all of this, namely that marriage should be indissoluble. First, in the Genesis text there is no mention of marriage as yet but only a growing existential bond expressed in the words 'cleave to' and 'become one flesh'. As we have already said, such a union is quite different in nature from a juridical bond like the one which constitutes marriage. Second, to support his views Jesus has recourse to the Bible which, as a Jew, he reads as infallible divine revelation. The modern believer cannot accept this. The surprising thing is that Jesus changes the sacred Genesis text on his own initiative to make it service his own argument. Nevertheless, his view remains important for us, even only for the reason that it is his. But in what way is he going beyond the Torah tradition? An important question, because, while the Torah can still inspire us it can no longer be binding.

Jesus goes beyond the Torah here in two ways. First, he rightly rejects the unilateral decision of the husband to end a marriage. He bursts the bubble of the divorce document because it is a legal fiction which does not remove the indissolubility of marriage. Second, more importantly he takes the discussion out of the juridical sphere. In the wake of the author of the Book of Genesis he penetrates to the core of the matter, to that which in his eyes is God's plan with the sexual encounter, namely the development of a deep and eventually unbreakable union. Every couple that marries dreams, consciously or unconsciously, of such a union, and this confirms without further proof or justification the profound validity of Jesus' view.

Thus Jesus interprets human sexuality as a call to existential union. In this union the creative evolution is revealed – and indeed as a movement which drives towards becoming 'one flesh'. Forming a bond with the partner is the beginning. This beginning calls for continuation. From this comes the obligation of the couple to do all in their power to realize the union. Here marriage is an aid. It serves to stop the couple from drifting apart. The breakdown of a marriage means that the call to existential union ends up fruitless and is blameworthy. The juridical prohibition of divorce, together with its sanctions, makes this censure socially palpable. But despite every help the existential unity, no matter how beautiful and touching the first steps were, can die. The juridical corset of marriage which remains after this death is then just as useless as the shell after the death of the organism which has formed the shell for its protection.

We can fully subscribe to Jesus' view of the profound meaning of forming a couple. Also to the resulting requirement that everything possible be done to promote the growing unity. This view represents great progress by comparison with the view of Torah, which clearly did not pursue any further the profound intuition of chapter 2 of the Book of Genesis. But Jesus still attempts to save the legal tradition of his people, probably because he is convinced that the Torah from which it originates is God's own word and therefore determines everything. In addition, he presents that tradition, with its prohibition of divorce (but without its being eased by the divorce certificate), as if it followed directly from his non-juridical view distilled from Genesis 2. But by no means does he do that. First, because in Genesis there is only talk of a process of becoming one, referred to by the author with the image 'becoming one flesh'. As yet there is no talk of marriage, which is the juridical time-conditioned structure meant to support this process. Second, because his argument that God Himself makes the (juridical) bond between man and woman has only the *appearance* of being biblical. It is his own addition to the Genesis text and thereby lacks the guarantee on which he tacitly depends. Third, because he has the Genesis text say what it in fact does not say. For in Genesis it is not God who would bind man and woman together – and indeed juridically – to provide the foundation for the indissolubility of marriage; it is the man himself who forms the existential bond with her, and indeed with a view to restoring the original unity with her. She came, namely, out of him, is flesh of his flesh as it says in Genesis 2:23, and precisely for this reason, says the text, he binds himself to her and not because God commanded it. As a consequence there is hardly anything left of the argument on which Jesus bases his prohibition of divorce.

A modern Christian also can say that God has bound a couple together if by that he means that fundamental love wants to express itself further, reveal itself, become palpable by bringing two human beings together to form an existential union. This union can, of course, only be formed by the couple itself. They join with one another. God does not do it without them. It is *their own* quite personal union. Once it has come about it is indissoluble by its very nature, for then the two have become genuinely 'one flesh'. But this union is not to be confused with the juridical indissolubility of a marriage, which belongs to a much lower plane. It is only a corset which one has buckled on as a protection of the existential union. This corset loses its meaning when the original and precious unity has died, for then there is nothing left to protect. Anyone who considers marriage binding even after the love has died out or, still worse, has turned into enmity, is merely propping up an empty juridical fiction.

Jesus' final words in no way mean that no human authority can juridically undo a knot which the parish priest (in the name of God?) has juridically tied. Besides, it is neither God nor the parish priest that legally binds the couple. The married couple do it themselves by their vows. At any rate in the registry office! But civil marriage and a Church marriage have an equal binding force. What is possible after a civil marriage is therefore also possible after a Church wedding, namely dissolution. Because Jesus is not speaking of a Church marriage but a Jewish one, which corresponds to our civil marriage, it would be better to omit from the marriage liturgy the words '... what God has put together ...'. Besides, a prohibition is not the same as an impossibility, or, in the official language of Canon Law: a forbidden act does not amount to an invalid act. The Church can forbid legally divorced people to marry again, but when they do it anyway the result is marriage and not concubinage.

Six consequences

Six findings result from the above considerations. Some of them can provoke resistance, but they are the logical consequences of a theonomous interpretation of the message to believers.

1. Where love has died, divorce is a fundamentally meaningful step. It is presupposed that there has been an honest and intensive attempt to keep love alive. But in most cases this has not happened. As a rule divorce is the regrettable result of an incapability or unwillingness to love unselfishly. It can be called the result of a 'hardness of heart' of which Jesus complains in Matthew 19:8, and which has choked the attempts to counteract the growing estrangement. What is blameworthy is not approaching the registry office or the courts, but much that has already happened. But even the *Catechism of the Catholic Church* acknowledges in no. 1649 that there are cases in which living together has become impossible in practice despite the best efforts of both parties. Documents from the early Middle Ages prove that it was permitted to such couples to regard their marriage as finished. Since the 9th century, however, the most that Church authorities permitted was that 'the married couple

be bodily separated', i.e. no longer share bed and board, but the authorities still wanted to keep up the fiction of a marriage. In reality they are concerned with an empty shell as if it was protecting some precious living thing. The cause of its concern is the mythical veneration of the Bible, all the words of which they take to be God's own words. It says in the Bible that marriage is indissoluble and that remarriage after divorce is adultery and therefore mortal sin. If, with modernity, we give up this mythological approach to the problem, the Church's view, together with the resulting practice, loses all foundation.

2. Despite all anathemas and excommunications, marrying again after a (registry office) divorce can be meaningful and good if the new couple is concerned, by this juridical step, to protect its desire for existential union. The Church authorities for their part are free not to acknowledge this new bond as marriage and to refuse to give Church approval to the new union through a liturgical ceremony. The question whether they are right in this, will be answered below. For lack of something better the marriage takes place in the registry office, but in the clear knowledge, perhaps contrary to the voice of the super-ego, that this in no way makes one into a public sinner, but that one is trying to take seriously the divine task of human development.

3. Indissolubility is seen in Church teaching as a quality inherent in marriage and therefore belonging to its essence. But what belongs to the essence of marriage can never disappear from it. This also leaves no room for the 'fornication clause' in Matthew 5:32. This is then an unbiblical interpolation of an error on the part of the evangelist. But Church tradition does not accept this. It has always considered the fornication clause as equally inspired as the indissolubility referred to in the same verse. The Orthodox Church has even based its own practice on this, which is different from that of the Catholic Church. It seems therefore more reasonable to accept that indissolubility is not a quality inherent in marriage. On top of this we can also refer here to the Pauline Privilege, which also contradicts the indissolubility of marriage. That deprives the Church of every basis for refusing to declare a marriage dissolved and null and void. When after protracted litigation, including the questioning of witnesses pro and contra, the Church courts are finally eager to determine (for a long time now at a cost) that a marriage has in fact never been a marriage, only a hidden concubinage, this is then only shadow-

boxing. Moreover, as a rule it was not a case of concubinage but a true marriage, i.e. a legally ratified honest decision and attempt to 'become one flesh'. The Church tribunal then really ratifies, with its declaration of invalidity, the sad end of a true marriage. In indignation the official Church judges will reject this view. They consider that death alone can end a marriage and that anyone who dares to marry again after civil divorce proceedings becomes thereby a public sinner. But that does not stand up to the criticism of the modern believer. Remarried divorcees are not greater sinners than other believers and therefore need no more pastoral care than other married people.

4. The indissoluble nature of marriage is often attributed, though incorrectly, to the sacramental character of a church marriage. That there is an error here is seen by the fact that the Church in the first thousand years of its history did not have a sacrament of marriage and yet for all that time, on the basis of the Bible, considered marriage indissoluble. It saw marriage as an indispensable social institution which gave order and structure to the cohabitation of its members. The sacrament of marriage has only been spoken about since the 13th century. Of course in the Bible, which the Church always invokes in matters of faith, there can be no mention of a sacrament of marriage, unless the Greek word *mysterion* in the letter to the Ephesians 5:32, which has been translated in the Vulgate as *sacramentum,* is wrongly interpreted as sacrament. Only in the course of the 12th century did the Church authorities begin to link the constituting of a marriage and its validity to a liturgical celebration and to prescribe for its validity the observance of strict rules. From that time, in the case of baptized Catholics, according to Canon Law a marriage only comes about when the couple, in making their mutual vows, observed all this rules. The strange results this can lead to can be seen from the following example: a couple has its marriage performed by a priest whom they have found ready to do it but who has not asked the parish priest of the groom or the bride for the necessary authority or jurisdiction to perform the marriage. According to the regulations he should have done this. Even if all other Church rules have been sedulously followed it is no use. There is no question of it being a marriage. The couple is living in concubinage. They just think they are married.

5. As we have seen, the Church authorities can refuse to recognize a civil marriage as marriage, but their refusal changes nothing of the social reality, since it is not the Church (any longer) that shapes this reality. A civil marriage fulfils all the requirements within our culture which make it possible to speak of marriage: namely, that a man and a woman, both single and able to marry, promise to one another in the presence of the empowered representative of society and two witnesses lasting fidelity. Likewise, the Church authorities can refuse divorcees a second church marriage, but if the views expressed in this chapter have also become the views of the couple, they have no particular reason to worry. Besides, not every Church official will, despite the official prohibition, shrink from incorporating the vows of such a couple into a church ceremony. The fact that this marriage is not entered into the church register of marriages, is only noticed by the paper on which it is not written! On the other hand, if people who are married in a church ceremony are asked their opinion about what exactly constitutes the sacrament of marriage which they have received, the answers as a rule are miles away from what is essential to a sacrament, namely a creative sign of the presence of the transcendent. For most people the ceremony is, above all, an enhancement of the wedding celebration. Such an enhancement is good in itself. But a sacrament is something different. And the 'validity' of a bond cannot depend on the level of solemnity of a ritual. Not a great deal is lost by the numerical decline in church weddings. Modern believers are clearly heading for a situation similar to that in the late Roman Empire. Marriage was not yet considered a sacrament and Christians married according to the custom of their culture, most of them *per usum*, i.e. by simply living together for a year and a day, the well-to-do *per coemptionem*, i.e. by agreement on a dowry.

6. One final comment concerns the overtones associated with the word adultery. This word sounds seriously reproachful. Probably this tone is due to the former connection with (mortal) sin and the threat of punishment in the afterlife. In itself this reproach is justified. But if it is to remain such in modernity the focus should be on the extra, superior value of love. For the modern believer love is not a secondary value. It is the ultimate value. Unrelated to love, this reproach is only the voice of the prohibiting super-ego, which is a carryover from the rejection of

sexual pleasure instilled in people by the Church. In that case the reproach bears no relation to the surrender in faith to the fundamental love of God which is at work in us. Most people also cannot say what would make adultery 'sinful'. They see it as only socially blameworthy. The euphemistic word 'fling' is a sign that what was earlier a serious condemnation of marital infidelity is now hardly more effective than a scarecrow. This fate is similar, indeed, to that of the entire pre-modern sexual ethics. For modern man a divine prohibition which belongs to the rarefied air of a supernatural world no longer has an impact. Yet adultery and marital infidelity are to be condemned. No longer, of course, because of a strict divine prohibition but as a serious breach of the loving intimacy built up and shared with the partner. This is an intra-mundane reality, the sacredness and inviolability of which needs no further discussion.

CHAPTER SIX

Renouncing Mammon

Pre-modern Christian ethics has been sadly lacking also in a second area and has thereby seriously hindered the humanization of the world, which is God's self-revelation: namely, where our beloved money is concerned. The consequences are still worse than those incurred by pre-modern sexual ethics. This latter was mainly injurious to personal growth. By comparison, the effects of pre-modern monetary ethics are socially devastating. The contrast, which at world level is crying out for revenge, between superfluity and want becomes hatred, becomes threat of terror, becomes mass migration, becomes a ruthless and compulsive drive. What is particularly bad here is that this contrast coincides with that between the Christian West and the deprived Third World. If in the Christian West the gospel, instead of greed, which is its direct opposite, had influenced economic activity, the world would not have come unstuck and we would have spared ourselves the current crisis. It is shameful for Christians that the monetary ethics of Islam is much more akin to the gospel, and therefore more promising for the future, than that of a Christianity in which the spirit of Mammon is more influential than the spirit of Jesus Christ.

It is worth noting that ownership is more a taboo area than sexuality. No one wants to be asked about his income and his money. This, too, is private, people say. Could it be that someone who has a lot wants to hide it from the gaze of his fellow men who are equally avaricious? Is he afraid that others, especially the authorities, would nibble away at his surplus if they were to find out how much it was? Even those who possess or earn a hundred times more than they need for living feel it deeply when they lose a few per cent of it. For what other reason do we see sportsmen, whose salaries amount to millions, moving to off-shore paradises? And where does the success of these tax paradises come from? And what is behind the attempts to protect bank secrecy from being relaxed? Would it not be better to slaughter this sacred cow? A person who has only a modest income normally does not look to manipulate his private financial affairs and reveals his earnings much more readily.

How have the Church authorities performed in the monetary sphere? Despite the similarity of this taboo area with the likewise taboo area of sexuality, both are in fact quite different. Just as severely as it has narrowed down any leeway in sexuality it has generously opened room to manoeuvre in ownership. This is quite worrying. For while in the words and actions of Jesus, which ought to be the source of our ethics, we find hardly anything which could justify puritanical views, by contrast, in his words and deeds he gives short shrift to every form of greed. He does not see wealth as a blessing but rather as a malady.

How are we to explain the worrying phenomenon that in the pre-modern Church ethics there is so much fuss about Venus and Amor while there is no problem with becoming friends of Mammon despite all Jesus' warnings? Perhaps this is the explanation: the people, more precisely, the men who developed those ethical laws and held them up to others were celibates. By punishing every form of freedom in the sexual sphere as a capital offence they were unconsciously trying to protect themselves from the tendency to yield to their unsatisfied sexual needs. Their tireless teaching that abstention was the only good way for the Christian was further reinforced in the Middle Ages by the success of monastic life which amazes us today. But at the same time the Church leaders were well-off, even rich, often stinking rich. Especially in Rome. And often as the fruit of pure simony. The sober diary of Johan Burchard, who was in 1500 the Master of Ceremonies at the court of the renaissance Pope Alexander VI, tells us – although it is not to be accepted unreservedly – much that is very interesting, yet hardly edifying. But Mammon was a welcome guest not just in Rome. What the archbishops of Salzburg or Würzburg, for example, left behind as witness to their luxury and their extravagant lifestyle is amazing. On top of that the powerful churchmen lived in a kind of symbiosis with the secular rulers. For the most part they came from these circles themselves and were natural friends and allies of the wealthy. Thus it was hardly likely that they would condemn wealth and preach the gospel of simplicity and frugality. They held up to their flock the 10 Commandments of the Old Testament, which is quite comfortable with wealth. But the words of Jesus, like those in Luke 12:15: 'Take heed and beware of all covetousness', just to name one of his statements, found only a very faint echo with these shepherds. In their preaching they preferred to steer clear of such words. However, covetousness is one of the so-called seven deadly sins, i.e. one of the seven sources of great harm and disaster in the world. In the traditional list of seven it is number two and is called avarice, often wrongly understood as the stinginess of a Scrooge in Dickens's *Christmas Carol*. This is not at all a mortal sin, but an unhealthy anomaly by which a person first and foremost makes *himself* unhappy. Avarice means greed, the desire to possess more and more. It is the materialistic deification of money. The miser prefers to spend nothing, if he can, while the greedy person wants to have as much as he can, to be able to spend at leisure. Only this avarice is a major sin. It bears the guilt of the hunger and the land grabbing and exploitation in the world, and this injustice is crying out for revenge. It has given birth to many a terrible economic crisis, the victims of which are the weak and the little people around the world. Furthermore, as the worship of money it is idolatry.

Just property and *un*just property

Is a Christian therefore not allowed to be rich? Of course he is, says the pre-modern pseudo-Christian ethics. There is such a thing as a right to property. And it is a sacred right. We have the sacred right to keep what we own, at least if it has not been acquired by dubious means. The Bible commands us to give alms occasionally (the Jews and the Muslims also have this command), but the very word alms is one we should find disgusting. While it suggests sympathy it is bathed in an atmosphere of pretension, makes the receiver dependent, humiliates him, factually denies him any right to the rich person's surplus, embodies and reinforces a power relationship. Added to this is the fact that the alms are mere crumbs that we drop from our overloaded table, keeping the poor person alive instead of fighting the causes of his poverty. After our alms-giving we can enjoy self-satisfaction and bask in the sunshine of our feeling of virtuousness and then with a good conscience go back to sit at our still fully-loaded table.

A Christian is therefore not allowed to be rich? Only, says the ethics of a modern believer, when his attitude is that of the property administrator, so that he lives with the awareness that he is less the owner than the trustee of what he has. His duty is to make sure that they profit from them, more than he does. It is namely peculiar to love (and the ethics of a modern believe is a love-ethics) that one shares with others what one has oneself. Together we are all cells in the great body of humanity. But cells communicate with one another. If in one part of humanity there is superfluity and in another there is privation, the surplus should flow naturally from one side to the other. But that does not happen. One of the reasons is that the owners call on a so-called right that pre-modern ethics defends tooth and nail: the (unlimited) right to property. The ethics of love does not speak of alms but of sharing. And as modern Christians we say with conviction that 'sharing with our brothers and sisters, that's what we have to do'. And that is what we think we are doing. But in reality we are still giving alms, giving up some of our surplus without genuinely sharing. Our right to property remains untouched by all that we give away. And our possessions remain our possessions.

The ethics of the modern believer also includes the idea of *un*just possession of property. Almost everyone who has much at his disposal, the well-off believer as well, will rear up against this idea. Our instinct to acquire possessions resists with all its might. We like very much to have plenty and a good conscience as well. And we have many arguments to hand to defend the status quo, no matter what the gospel says. Also, no matter what love says. And we feel that we are strongly supported by the supernatural ethics in which we have been educated. Having no right to property is in that context an unfamiliar expression.

Where does right to property become transformed into injustice? Where I keep for myself what I absolutely do not need while I could use it to alleviate somewhat the dire need of my fellow men. How that can work in the concrete is shown by an evangelically inspired organization in Flanders, which calls itself (here translated) 'Modest for Others'. Each member is to decide for himself what he needs to live in moderate comfort. How much someone needs for this is a matter for the person to decide for himself and depends on numerous factors. No one can make this decision for others. Furthermore, each should cover himself with the necessary insurances and likewise put aside a modest reserve for unforeseen events. Everyone can make a just claim to

dispose of all this, but not to all that goes beyond this. This is
where the injustice of property begins. What one has or earns
over and above that just claim rightly belongs to those who do
not have enough to live by. In accordance with the laws of
communicating pipes the personal surplus should flow to these
persons, and not as alms but as something to which they have a
right. And when someone has shared in this way he should not
puff himself up as if he had done anything special, for then the
sobering word of Jesus is to hand in Luke 17:10: 'When you have
done all that has been commanded, then say: we have only done
that which we ought to do.'

Anyone whose starting point is the ethics of love can only
subscribe to what the organization 'Modest for Others' says and
does, even though for most people it goes against the grain.
Thinking in quite practical terms and supposing, for the time
being, that lotteries were to be ethically acceptable (soon it will
be made clear that they are at the very least suspect), we have to
come to this conclusion: anyone who already lives in very comfortable circumstances and wins 100,000 Euro in such a game of
chance has, for a modern believer, no right to this money. He
only has the right to decide how to use it for the good of those
people who on the basis of their plight have need of it. The
situation where help is required is not necessarily a material one.
Nor is simply giving the money away the only solution. There are
other intelligent ways to help. But in whatever way it may
happen, the money no longer belongs to the winner. No more
than a bank employee can regard as his own and use for himself
all the money that goes through his hands every day. The money
belongs to others. And he will have to give an account of how he
has handled the money. If he forgets this he will be a thief, just as
much as the person who steals.

Probably some readers will have frowned in disapproval at the
suggestion that games of chance where large sums of money are
involved should be considered wrong on ethical grounds. What is
so wrong with these games of chance? That they are aimed at
stimulating our innate greed. And that Jesus has no good word to
say for greed. Even praiseworthy intentions – which by the way
seldom play a role – as, for example, to support social projects
with the winnings, have as their dark side the fact that through
participation we contribute to the success of this cult. Anyone
who is not worried by greed will merely shrug on hearing this

argument. Some time ago there was an advertising slogan in Germany and Austria: 'Greed is great!' And unfortunately the greater majority of baptized people in Western society consciously or unconsciously agree and thereby prove that their Christianity is little more than a coat of varnish, for, to whitewash greed – to say nothing of praising it – flatly contradicts Jesus' view, which is precisely the norm for Christian ethics. For Jesus is the purest revelation of the fundamental love which is God. The fact that Jesus condemns all forms of greed is to most Christians unfortunately of no significance. Representatives of a party with a Christian emblem consider that it is in no way incompatible with their profession of faith in Jesus Christ to swell their already handsome salaries as representatives or government ministers by feeding out of three, five or ten other troughs. Or think of the success of the television programmes in which the demonstration of useless knowledge is rewarded with the payment of umpteen thousand Euro. The avid interest of hundreds of thousands of viewers, as the candidates take on, step by step, increasingly difficult tasks for higher amounts of money, is the writing on the wall. It manifests confirmation by the audience that 'greed is great'. And the audience is for the most part made up of the baptized. And few active church members say a resolute no to such programmes, whereas they would write letters of protest if anything which they judge to be pornographic were to appear on the screen. Is the second deadly sin therefore an innocent pastime by comparison with the third? In this way the Church harvests the sour grapes of an ethical teaching which has put the emphasis where it does not belong, namely on sexuality, and has trivialized greed, which is the really anti-evangelical and deadly sin. It is not surprising that a Christianity which hardly takes the gospel of Jesus Christ seriously is in no position to resist the onslaught of forces in Western society which threaten to sweep it aside.

This society is undoubtedly also characterized by elements which originate in the gospel. The Church has for a thousand years handed on much of it and thereby prevented the person and words of Jesus being lost in oblivion. In non-Christian societies these elements are not found, or at least not to the same extent. This is true with regard to care for disadvantaged or disabled people. But from the lack of Church preaching, where there was blindness in this particular eye, the rejection of every form of greed did not take hold in Western society. A Christianity which Jesus need not be ashamed of must therefore swim against the tide in today's society and even in the Church of today.

Just inheritance and unjust inheritance

This need to swim against the tide applies likewise to the right to inheritance which is accepted without qualms. The Church's preaching has lulled us to sleep also in this sphere. It has not drawn our attention to the fact that in the prosperous West it would be more to the point (not always!) to speak of what is in fact *unjust* inheritance instead of the right to inheritance. Naturally, not 'just or unjust' in the eyes of society, precisely because the gospel has no influence on their views. And it has no influence, because in the pulpit there has always been silence about the proper Christian attitude towards inheritance. And this silence has been wrong. Inheritance is a very dubious business from a Christian point of view. First, it is often the cause of bitter division and lasting feuds between brothers and sisters. But divisions and feuds are in complete contradiction to the repeated and pressing calls of Jesus to forgive and be reconciled. Besides, they are a bad sign that, for so-called Christians, possession and therefore greed is more important than the most fundamental command of their faith: love. But even where everything has been settled and divided up peacefully, in many cases the question remains whether inheritance is compatible with the faith we profess. This question has been clarified above where the legitimacy of ownership was discussed. The limits of this legitimacy were outlined in the course of introducing the organization 'Modest for Others'. Anyone who possesses more than he needs for living in modestly comfortable circumstances, who has covered himself with the help of insurances and has a suitable reserve as a cushion against unforeseen accidents, can no longer lay just claim to the additional umpteen thousand Euro which fall into his lap through inheritance. He has to decide in what way he will serve with this additional money the just interests of the needy here and elsewhere.

For his part the testator should, in line with evangelical logic, while sharing out his possessions, have more left over for those in need of help. But in the meantime the words of Jesus that we should not gather treasures where the moth and the worm destroy and where thieves break in and steal, are for him obviously gone with the wind. That a single old woman leaves ten million Euro in her will for good causes (this is an actual case) is of course praiseworthy. But why did she wait until she died? A small fraction of this would have been plenty to deal comfortably with the unforeseeable events of old age. In the meantime people had to live for years in wretched circumstances, whereas this money locked up in her bank vault could have enabled them to have a dignified human existence.

The situation is naturally different in the bequeathing of a business or an enterprise. Such a bequest has a social function for the benefit of many – in the first place, the workers. It is more a responsibility than an enrichment. The heir should manage it with care and not just give it up or share it out, but use it as an ongoing source of income through which he can come to the aid of the needy part of the world. But the golden rule of the organization 'Modest for Others' remains in force. In itself, there is nothing wrong with being as rich as Bill Gates, if one regards only that little bit as one's rightful possession which is necessary for living in modest comfort and dedicates the (sometimes hundred-fold greater) remainder to the common good, and most especially to the good of the many who are badly off.

Utopian perhaps, but in any case a blessing

It is to be expected that there will be strong resistance to this evangelical view of things. Not only in materialist circles but also where Christians in the secret recesses of their heart have built a little altar in honour of holy Mammon. Even loyal Church-goers will be vigorously opposed to this view. Our Church ethic is a law-based ethic, and Canon Law nowhere demands that we act like this. The right to property and the right to inheritance are here undisputed. But love goes further than the law. And the ethics of the modern believer is an ethics based on love.

Yet the world and the Church are so much at odds with this in their thinking that it is utopian to expect this dream of a no longer avaricious humanity to be realized even in the distant future. In the Acts of the Apostles 2:44-46 and 4:3 this utopia is indeed described as realized in the early Church: 'All who had become believers formed a community and owned everything in common. They sold their possessions and gave of them to all, each according to his need.' But that is very probably a pious idealization and the actual reality only partly corresponded to this ideal picture, as the story of Ananias and Saphira shows.

However, in church history something of this ideal has always remained in evidence. It took on a concrete form in monastic communities, since there everything (in principle) is owned in common and everyone lives according to the Marxist but fundamentally Christian ground rule: 'Everyone works according to his ability and receives according to his needs.' And this principle has shown its sustainability, for it is still alive after more than 1500 years. Also in the so-called Reductions of the Jesuits in Paraguay in the 17th and 18th centuries the Indians lived according to the above-mentioned ground rule. Those in command took care that every Indian in the Reduction had enough and no one had too much. Today the Hutterite Brothers, the Anabaptist community founded by the South Tirolean Jakob Hutter in 1528 as a movement returning to the pure gospel of Jesus Christ, still live according to this ideal of ownership in common in the spirit of the gospel. They were soon persecuted and driven away by the Habsburgs – Hutter himself was imprisoned, cruelly tortured and in 1536 died at the stake in front of the Goldenes Dachel in Innsbruck – and were expelled again and again, also by other Catholic princes because of their fidelity to the gospel (which was uncomfortable for the princes). The Hutterites finally emigrated to Canada. Their 'farms' as their communities are called, can be thought of as monasteries without celibacy.

Marxism also was an attempt, in much greater measure than previously, to put an end to the scandalously unjust distribution of earthly goods. But since compulsion took over instead of love, the attempt was doomed to fail. As long as slogans like 'possession is possession' and 'greed is great' set the tone, the chances of there being an evangelical attitude towards possessions are slim, both worldwide and throughout the Church. The modern Christian whose motto is 'Modest for Others' will therefore try to achieve something on a smaller sale. And by contrast to the idealized church of the Acts of the Apostles he will no longer be concerned to alleviate, by a form of common possession of goods, the needs of his fellow believers.

Instead, his ground rule is that of the communicating pipes: 'My too much simply wants to go where there is too little.'

CHAPTER SEVEN

The Tension between Obedience and Freedom

The difference between a modern believer's ethics and pre-modern ethics also becomes apparent in the relationship between obedience and freedom. By their very nature there is a relationship of tension between the two. This is one form of the typically human tension between community and person. It is foreign to the animal kingdom, where the individual does not stand out from the collective. But humanity is not a herd or horde or anthill. Each human being is a person with inalienable rights. The indispensable obedience, to the totality of which he is a part and on which he depends and without which he cannot exist, has to be brought into harmony with this. This harmony is what enables him to live a meaningful life. If freedom always claims the lion's share for itself, the result is life-threatening chaos. If obedience has the first and last word and almost all words between, the result is inhuman slavery. Neither of the above can promote the growth of the Kingdom of God.

Obedience at the cost of freedom?

Unfortunately, in the Church freedom has only too often been sacrificed on the altar of obedience in honour of God-in-Heaven. In this context obedience has almost been elevated to the rank of the prime virtue. If a Catholic does not want to endanger his salvation, he should believe all that the Church authorities present him with and do everything they prescribe for him to do. Obedience has, furthermore, become one of the three main pillars of monastic life – that style of life which tradition recognizes as especially laudable, almost as ideal.

We could consider this emphasis on obedience as an obvious consequence of the social character of the Church in general and of monastic life in particular. All corporate bodies, like an army or a choir or a football team, can only keep functioning properly thanks to an organizing authority and the corresponding obedience it requires. Collaboration and living together become impossible if each individual only does what he likes. The Abbey of Thélème, where the motto was: 'Do what you like', could only exist in the comical imagination of a Rabelais.

The Church, too, is unthinkable without authority. But for its claim to obedience the pre-modern Church authorities did appeal to something quite different from this sociological necessity. Their right to command and the corresponding duty of the Church members to listen to them, they saw as a mandate from God. When Rome speaks God speaks through them, they maintain. Hence the saying: *Roma locuta, causa finita*: if Rome has spoken, that is the end of the matter. And so God Himself appears on stage. Any appeal to a higher authority is *a priori* excluded. There *is* no higher authority. Confronted with the absolute, everything human is, according to Isaiah 40:15 'nothing more than a drop in the bucket, a speck of dust on the scales'. This absolute authority has sent Jesus into the world and, according to the words in Matthew 28:12, 'given him all power on heaven and on earth'. This power, and therefore the right to command and to demand obedience, was then given by Jesus to Peter. We are meant to accept in good faith that this handing over really happened, no matter how much there is to the contrary. In any case the texts used to prove the papal succession convince only those who are already convinced. Depending, namely, on whether the biblical scholar is Roman Catholic or Evangelical, objective study leads him to surprisingly contrasting results. Peter would have handed on his authority to his successor, who is completely unknown to us, and this one to the next in a series down to the 266th, in 2016 Franciscus. It is true that none of these successors personally handed on this authority. Each was long since dead and buried when his successor assumed office. How the successor was given the authority remains an open question. Rome can always invoke the words Luke 10:16 ascribes to Jesus: 'Whoever listens to you (i.e. the Church authorities) listens to me.' Through these authorities, equipped now with his own divine power, Jesus himself speaks, binding (and loosing) and infallible. Anyone who says no to a Vatican prescription therefore says no to God. Also anyone who says no to an episcopal directive says no to God, for bishops have, if only in a reduced form, a share in the fullness of divine authority which all the successors of Peter can invoke. To obey these prescriptions is therefore the only path to the salvation offered by God.

But what is here called obedience hides in reality something else, namely subjection as a product of fear instilled in people by the Church authorities using the threat of punishment. In earlier days the authorities were able to make their subjects feel these punishments in their own flesh. And if the guilty person managed to escape by the skin of his teeth, justice in the other world awaited him. And the punishment that awaited him would be no laughing matter.

When the Church authorities demand obedience there is definitely an element of genuine concern for the unity of the Church, which was close to Jesus' heart, as his parting speech in John's gospel confirms. Therefore, not 'do as you like', for otherwise in the end there will be nothing left of this unity. But an obedience which is fundamentally nothing more than submissiveness produces uniformity more than unity. Uniformity certainly has its advantages. It strengthens the socio-logical cohesion of a group and gives it a clear profile, thereby increasing its chances of survival against competition. But uniformity is still not unity. Unity is an inner bond which can quite well go hand in hand with a plurality of forms, which is more an enrichment than a threat. Every human experience of the divine is limited and thereby one-sided and inadequate, because every person experiences that inexhaustible richness differently. Encountering the difference of the experience which others have protects us from reducing the Fundamental Mystery to the dimensions of our own experience and seeing our own experience of God as the only right one. Besides, the Roman Catholic Church, despite all its uniformity, is not at all a model of unity. Leadership and grassroots are living in fact in a horizontal schism. A considerable part of the grassroots thinks and acts differently in things which the leadership considers particularly important and does not shy away from ignoring the pertinent prescriptions which come from Rome. One can think of ecumenism, the priesthood, priestly celibacy, equality of women, birth control, euthanasia, the right of the grassroots to be heard.

The Bible supports freedom

Submissiveness is the product of fear of another person's weapons or of the voice of the super-ego built into us by our education. True obedience begins when we listen to another voice, the voice of the absolute. This absolute does not compel us, nor does it come to us from outside. It coincides with our inner-most being. Our freedom consists precisely in our ability to listen to this voice deep within us and to act in accordance with it. Submissiveness eliminates this freedom to which we are called as human beings and even more as Christians. If it is permissible to listen to human commands, this is only because, and insofar as, we hear in them the voice of the absolute. This is the voice of the true and the good. If human directives and prohibitions contradict this voice we should say a definite no. We are not allowed to give up the divine gift of freedom in order to dance to the tune of human beings. We would demean ourselves as persons and be standing in the way of the divine evolutionary movement which presses on to further humanization. This would be especially taboo for Christians. To be a Christian requires that we follow in the steps of Jesus, who was a uniquely free and liberating person. As Christians we should take the task of living in as humanly dignified a way as possible even more seriously than does the modern humanist non-believer. We should recognize a Christian by the fact that he is a free person who is only led by the voice he hears deep within himself, God's voice which drives him towards all that is true and good and beautiful.

Witnesses in the oldest tradition, recorded in the New Testament, leave no room for doubt in this regard. It is possible to compile a litany of such witnesses, for example: The spirit of the Lord has sent me to set at liberty those that are bruised (Luke 4:19); delivered into the liberty of the glory of God (Romans 8:21); but now we are loosed from the law of death (Romans 7:6); why is my liberty judged by another man's conscience? (1 Corinthians 10:29); where the spirit of the Lord is there is liberty (2 Corinthians 3:17); the freedom we have in Jesus Christ (Galatians 2:4); be not held again under the yoke of bondage (Galatians 5:1); for you, brethren, have been called unto liberty (Galatians 5:13); the perfect law of liberty (James 2:12); act as free men (1 Peter 2:16).

When in the hymn in chapter 2 of the letter to the Philippians Paul praises the obedience of Jesus, he is clearly dealing with Jesus' obedience to God and not to human authorities. It is this obedience which is our model, not his willing obedience as a child in Luke 2:51. That is, by the way, the only instance in the Bible where Jesus is seen as obeying human beings. In his letter to the Romans 13:1 Paul does require of his followers that they obey the ruling powers, i.e. human beings, but only because in his view they represent God. Such obedience naturally ceases when the state demands things which contradict the voice of the absolute.

With the words freedom and liberation we arrive at the core of the Christian message. 'Redemption', a key word and an ever recurring theme in this message, is only an old-fashioned Church synonym for liberation. Therefore freedom in thinking and acting is more Christian than the submissiveness adorned with the name of obedience. Despite the array of witnesses attesting to freedom, we only seldom hear from the part of Church authorities, which are otherwise always invoking the Bible, a call to think and act freely. Perhaps out of the not unfounded fear that the faithful will use the concept freedom as a cover-up for caprice and vain-glorious behaviour. Paul had also given expression to this fear and warned of the danger of giving scandal, by one's own freer behaviour, to those who were weaker in faith. Precisely that two-fold fear has resulted in the never-ending emphasis on submission being converted into an uncritical following of prescriptions. The motto 'orders are orders' was not only taught and practised in the army. The Church authorities were successful in this regard because they considered themselves to be the authoritative mouthpiece of the divine voice and were considered and revered as such by the members of the Church. And the belief that they were really God's mouthpiece, was (not without coercive measures) transmitted from generation to generation right down to the present day.

For modern believers, what is the authority of the hierarchy based on?

But if the whole second world is a *fata morgana*, as modernity sees it, all the claims of popes and bishops to obedience lose their foundation. Then those Excellencies and Eminences who were until recently clad in divine authority, are standing there like the emperor in Anderson's fairy tale with no clothes on. They may be richer (at least they used to be) or more learned (occasionally they are) than their 'sheep' or subjects, but in essence they are only fellow human beings. To subordinate oneself to a fellow human being to whom we are essentially equal, is contrary to human dignity, because it is the attitude of a slave, not that of a free man. We can only be dictated to, without loss of status, by the true and the good. Here we are not on the same level. It transcends us, because in it God, the ultimate reality, is speaking. Only God is greater than human freedom, which is only a spark struck from his absolute freedom.

Does that mean that because of that *fata morgana* the hierarchy of pope and bishops no longer has any authority? Can they no longer issue any binding commands? Do we no longer need to heed them? God forbid! No, the hierarchy is invested with authority. But it does not come from a world on high. It comes from the community. The community, the whole, is namely greater than each of its parts, because it transcends them. The totality, however, speaks and administers through those parts which it has appointed to speak for it. But how are they appointed? No longer from on high, which in modernity does not exist anymore. The Church authorities no longer have political power through which they could give the illusion of authority and bring about submission with the use of force. The only way left is the democratic one based on the voice of the grassroots. But democracy is the child of a modernity which is still suspect in the Church and is thereby a bugbear for the hierarchy. That all power comes from the people, a sentence which has a prominent place in the constitution of many modern states, was always seen in the pre-modern Church as godless, because in its view all power comes from God-in-Heaven. But for a modern-thinking Church it comes from the community, which alone can empower someone to issue prescriptions and orders for the good of the whole. The leadership is never allowed to behave as lord and master of the community. The latter is and remains *their* lord and master. As soon as their voice is no longer recognizable as the voice of the whole it is usurping authority.

But the Church as a community is not like any other. Its essential characteristic is that the spirit of Jesus Christ penetrates it and holds it together. It is namely the gathering of those who have let this Jesus speak to them, whom he attracts, influences spiritually, transforms somewhat, so that they become more like him and so that his presence in them can become visible. On the basis of the presence of this living Jesus in the faithful who are inspired by him the Church can be called the Jesus who lives on in history, or, in the language of the Church, his body. Just like every corporate entity, this body produces organs for its preservation and growth, as well as forms of leadership. These forms owe their authority entirely to the body that produced them, and therefore ultimately to the living Jesus. Their task consists therefore in reminding the members of the essential demands their faith in Jesus makes on them, the most important of these being love of their fellow man. What this love means concretely for a Christian we learn from the gospel and from the example of the many who have gone before us on this path. The leadership should continually remind its members of these demands. And the members should listen. Real obedience consists in this listening. Then we are no longer obeying human beings but Jesus who is alive in the Church, according to the words quoted above from Luke 10:16. His spirit is the touchstone of all Church prescriptions, of Church dignitaries' decisions, and of Canon Law. Anything that does not pass this test has no value or binding power – which could be true of many existing regulations.

The difficult synthesis of obedience and freedom for believers

For the modern believer the mark of an authentic Christian is not at all seen as obedience to the pope and the bishops, but as obedience to the voice of love. The Christian should therefore never ask whether anything is permitted, i.e. allowed by Rome or the bishop. He should ask whether it is good, whether it promotes the common good, whether love calls for it. And if his own insight is not sufficient to show him what he should do, there are enough other believers whose worthy lives can teach him. Perhaps this will bring him into conflict with the leadership and with those who follow the leadership through thick and thin. But then the words from the Acts of the Apostles 5:29 apply, that one must obey God rather than man, and therefore listen to the voice of the Fundamental Love in us, which we hear in the voice of Jesus Christ, rather than to another voice which is still called Church authority but is in fact ecclesiastical power. Church leadership does have full authority to give direction when it expresses what is demanded by the good of the whole. But the grassroots, who in the meantime have found their voice, often know this quite as well as does the leadership – which also must listen to the Church members' own experiences of the divine. This view was confirmed in principle in Vatican Council Two but never resulted in practical decisions.

On the other hand it is right for a believer to acknowledge the authority of the Church to give direction, even though the modern believer cannot agree with the way in which the Church leaders are appointed. In modernity the only feasible method is the democratic vote. But this does not exist in the Church. The choice of pope is the nearest thing to a democratic process. But this process is skewed from the outset. The voters themselves are not chosen by the community. They are named by the previous autocratic ruler. And for his authority the newly chosen holy monarch invokes the authority communicated to him from above. For modernity, however, this means that his authority comes from 'nothing'. On the basis of such authority, which isn't one, the pope appoints bishops whose authority likewise has no foundation.

Should we then listen to Church leaders who base their authority on an imaginary mandate from God-in-Heaven? Of course we should. But not because of this claim, but because the Church membership to which we belong, accepts and affirms them for whatever reason. This affirmation by the community has the same value as a vote. Even if we completely disagree with the totally undemocratic method of appointing these Church officials, once they have been accepted by the members, we should acknowledge their authority and power to command. Our concern for the good of the totality is concretized then in our readiness to listen to them, for they duly represent this totality. But what is good and true must be more important to us than their person and their function. Where they exceed their authority, the mantle of love spread over everything will become a form of dishonesty. And to listen to them even then will become disobedience to the voice of God in our inner depths. Because the leadership then loses the right to obedience, it becomes a simple member of the whole, just like other members. To submit to it would mean denying the sacred gift of freedom.

The papacy

In the Church, the authority which can demand obedience is the hierarchy, literally 'holy administrative power'. This has a twofold division: the pope and the bishops. Both functions have gone through an astounding and hardly evangelical development. There is no longer a hint of service and modesty connected with these names, but rather a hint of superiority and power. Since modernity with its ideals of liberty, equality and fraternity dissolved mediaeval culture, much of this development seems regrettable in the eyes of today's believers. This is especially true of the papacy.

By papacy we mean here the historically developed absolute position of power of the bishop of Rome within the Roman Catholic Church. This historically developed papacy is something quite different from the Petrine ministry or the function which Peter performed in the four gospels as *primus inter pares*, the first among equals. The bishops of Rome claim this role for themselves on the basis of their claim to be the successors of Peter and heirs to his mandate. But Jesus was not thinking of a long history for his group of followers and therefore for successors to Peter either. He was convinced that the Kingdom of God would be coming soon. Twenty-five years later Paul and the early Church were still thinking the same. But since the end they were looking forward to, did not come about and the number of Eastern Churches was steadily increasing, there was a need for unity in all that diversity and along with that came the awareness of the need for a ministry to represent this unity and to guarantee its survival. The successor in Rome's primacy cannot invoke the historical Jesus. It was a product of believers' human understanding.

What began as Petrine ministry gradually developed in the course of the centuries into the papacy, and that means: an absolute monarchy. Canon 333 of the Codex of Canon Law adjudges that the pope has all power within the Church: legislative, administrative and juridical and without there being any possibility of appeal against a papal decision. This concentration of powers is characteristic of absolute monarchies and dictatorships, whereas the *division* of these powers is characteristic of democracy. For the exercise of his power the pope has at his disposal ministries, councils, functionaries, embassies and diplomatic services, a mini-state, a bodyguard, and especially the requisite enormous capital in the form of shares and deposits. Peter would be stunned if he came back and saw what had come out of his modest work as *primus inter pares*, as the first among equals. There is not the slightest sign of equality to be seen.

Does this development then have no good sides? Of course it has some. Despite all the unevangelical things that followed, the favour of the Roman emperors opened up for the Church possibilities of expansion and growth which it would otherwise not have had. The power of the papacy has also given the Church a voice with which it can let an evangelical message resound in the chaotic world of our day. Today the popes enjoy enormous prestige in the outside world, in politics and business, and that can only benefit the further development of mankind.

However, this development is and remains a wrong kind of development. Can anything be done about it? Not much, unfortunately. We can only review our own attitude towards the papacy by seeing in the pope only the man who plays Peter's role. Only as such is he important and even necessary. We should say no to everything which contradicts this Petrine ministry and therefore refuse to go along with a veneration which is seen in expressions like 'His Holiness the Pope' or 'the Holy Father'. And stop busying ourselves with encyclicals, conclaves, consistories, papal speeches, naming of cardinals and papal nuncios, television appearances, biographies of popes, the pope's sicknesses and accidents, the pope's journeys and pilgrimages and holidays. The almost hysterical veneration of the pope which is strongly encouraged by the media does not have much to do with Jesus. And it certainly has nothing to do with Peter. Why then for his 266th successor? Today's veneration of the pope is not a personal cult. It is the honouring of a function which promises the faithful security in a world where insecurity is rampant. But that is not where we should expect to find security, but in God alone. The Old Testament prophets and Books of Wisdom remind us of this in many texts. It is therefore a Christian duty to oppose the

honouring of that function which is a malformation of the true
Petrine ministry.

The role of the pope within the Church should be newly
defined today and in such a way that the papacy becomes a
Petrine ministry again. A comparison with the function of
General Secretary of the UNO could help to show the way. This
General Secretary plays an important role as representative of a
worldwide organization which is irreplaceable in its work for the
good of humanity. From this function the General Secretary
derives his authority, which is not power but the right to lift up
his voice and be heard. And his word has weight. But he is not
honoured as a divine phenomenon, and what he says is not seen
as infallible, and where he appears there are no gatherings of
hundreds of thousands of people with jubilant acclamations. In
ancient Rome during the triumphal processions a slave was
always to stand behind the triumphant victor on his chariot and
was to say to him from time to time: 'Remember that you are
(only) a human being!' Perhaps it would not be such a bad idea to
have one of the many cardinals play a similar role for the pope on
his white pope mobile.

The office of bishop

In the modern believer's world the function and authority of
bishops also appear in a different light from previously. In the
pre-modern view a bishop is a man invested with an exclusive
right from on high to consecrate churches and altars, to
administer confirmations, to ordain priests, i.e. to perform acts
which exclusively belong to a supernatural world. Along with this
he has been allotted the duty, by God-in-Heaven and through the
pope, of ruling people in a particular territory, teaching them and
if necessary punishing them. The believers then have the
obligation, on foot of this divine decision, to listen to him and to
do what he says. Since the disappearance of that supernatural
world all of this becomes untenable. It was made clear above why
a modern believer should still acknowledge a cleric who has
suddenly been promoted to bishop as someone invested with
administrative power, namely because the community of believers to which he belongs has accepted him as their bishop. They
have thereby invested him with legitimate authority.

The bishops claim that they are successors to the apostles. Bishop Irenaeus of Lyon said this for the first time 1800 years ago, and since then each one has repeated it after him. Historically it is not possible to speak of such a succession. Impartial historians of the early Church make this clear, as did von Harnack more than 100 years ago. But something that is repeated a thousand-fold ends up by being bathed in an aura of uncontested truth. And the bishops like this error very much. It sustains their importance. What is historically sound is the probability that at the beginning of the Church there were only collective forms of local leadership. The leadership was comprised of a committee of so-called elders or *episkopoi*, literally supervisors. Gradually it came about that the local leadership consisted of just one *episkopos*. Originally this *episkopos* was what we can anachronistically call the parish priest of a small community. This is clear from the letters to Timothy and to Titus. We can see there what conditions he had to meet. Amongst other things he was to have a wife and children. Historical circumstances, above all the mediaeval alliance between the Church and political power and the steadily developing growth in population, have gradually turned the priest in charge of a small parish into a powerful political figure, often a territorial lord, a prince, and, within his now often gigantic diocese, a lord and master.

This has also had consequences for his function. The *episkopoi* in the early stages of the Church's development could, in the language of the culture of the time, rightly be called shepherds. Today's bishops also call themselves shepherds; they write pastoral letters and stride along majestically with the crozier, which was originally a stick bent in such a way that the shepherd could take the sheep by the foot if it wanted to escape. Thus it is a symbol of power. But the biblical images of the flock and the shepherd have had their day. They belong to a nomadic culture which is long since passed. Today they can only meet with rejection because 'flock' conjures up the notion of immaturity and 'shepherd' evokes the notion of paternalism. But that is not the only reason why the bishops should no longer call themselves shepherds. A shepherd knows his sheep, but the bishop knows only a few of the hundreds of thousands or even millions that make up his 'flock'. Can a million sheep still be called a flock and the man responsible for this million a shepherd?

Today's bishop, in contrast to the earlier *episkopos*, is less a pastor than an administrator. Administration is also indispensable. But the real pastors of the diocese are the parish priests and deacons and pastoral helpers. They do the real pastoral work, which is much more important than the administrative work. The bishop should then not see them as his subordinates who do the work which he should do himself, but cannot do because of the time and effort it takes to administer everything. He should see himself with regard to them as a *primus inter pares*, as the first amongst equals, as the deans do in the superintendent's district. This means also that, just like the deans, he should look after his own parish and not leave it in the care of a so-called cathedral prelate. It is clear that he does not have time because of the enormous size to which his predecessors allowed the originally small parish to grow instead of continually dividing it up into new parishes, each with its own *episkopos*. The future will tell whether this process is irreversible.

What remains of the office of bishop if its supernatural garb is put aside – not just the mitre and crozier, but also the whole conception of his role which developed in the course of the Middle Ages? Just the man (for the time being, still not a woman) at the head of a manageable community, who according to Mark 10:44 should not be his Excellency or Eminence or Monsignor, but the servant of all.

CHAPTER EIGHT

Euthanasia

In recent years the Church authorities have again and again voiced their opinions on bioethical issues, a sign that it considers bioethics to be very important. And it has not been sparing with its condemnations. These condemnations concern, as well as the use of contraceptives (their pronouncements regarding the condom in the fight against AIDS can serve as an example), above all, abortion, artificial insemination (IVF: in vitro fertilization), and euthanasia. On each of these controversial points the Church sees with indignation that in Western society the flood of deviating views is rapidly rising. Its own ethical stance is naturally that of pre-modern ethics, which does not necessarily mean that in their thinking they are on the wrong track; but the ethics of a modern believer can come to other conclusions on certain points. Because of the limited scope of this book, Chapter Eight will deal with only one of the four themes: euthanasia. After a clear definition of the concept, which is essential for avoiding misunderstandings, and a brief historical survey of the problem, the positions and arguments of non-believing modern humanism and those of pre-modern believers and finally the view of a modern believer will be presented.

Introduction

Euthanasia is understood here as the intentional ending of a life, not by the person in question – that would be suicide, not euthanasia – but by another person, although at the request of the person in question. While in Western society the affirmation of euthanasia is gradually growing, the Church authorities invoke tradition and continue to condemn it. Even the ethical validity of refusing or discontinuing procedures for lengthening life – such as operations, the use of a breathing apparatus, artificial feeding where there is a continuing vegetative state – is contested by the Church. The council for medical ethics and the medical faculty of the (Catholic) University of Louvain considers that to turn off a breathing apparatus or to cease feeding through a tube is completely ethically justified. But Church authorities continue to condemn these practices, as in the recent case of the Italian Eluana Englaro, whose father had urgently requested that after 17 years in a coma she no longer be fed artificially, and in the case of the paralysed Giorgio Welby at whose request the breathing apparatus was turned off and who was then, as a 'suicide', refused a Church burial.

Etymologically the word euthanasia contains the two Greek roots *eu*, good, well, and *than-*: death. It should therefore mean 'good dying', a death in the best possible circumstances, i.e. with as little pain and fear as possible and with as much consciousness as possible, which is exactly the aim of palliative medicine. But in today's parlance euthanasia suggests an action which puts an end to suffering experienced as unbearable and thereby in fact eliminates palliative medicine.

The debate about euthanasia became a current issue only late in the second half of the previous century. Until then euthanasia was never talked about. The word used to evoke the dreadful memories of how the Nazi regime handled the disabled and other forms of 'worthless' life. Only in 1970 did people begin in the Netherlands to discuss the theme. In modern-thinking circles the idea of euthanasia was gradually entertained. But at the same time it caused the Church authorities to enter the fray. And public opinion also showed little inclination to accept it. But in the last two decades there has been a turnaround. Cases like that of Giorgio Welby and Eluana Englaro in Italy and Chantal Sébire in France, talked up by the media, played an important role here. Questionnaires in France showed that the number of those in favour of euthanasia was increasing by leaps and bounds after the horribly disfigured face of Chantal Sébire was shown on television. This affirmation of euthanasia was dictated above all by emotion, but emotions are by their very nature passing and are not reliable sources of advice.

In what follows, the legal aspect of euthanasia will deliberately be left out of the discussion. Legal directives are necessary to prevent abuses which flourish when rather than the good of the suffering person one's own advantage is sought, for instance when one wants to be free of the burden and expense which the prolonging of life imposes on the relatives, or to come more quickly into possession of an inheritance. Here it is exclusively a question of an ethical judgement of actions which can be labelled as killing but which in particular countries are already deemed legal. Belgian law, for instance, permits that 'a doctor whose patient is incurably sick and in unbearable pain, and who has freely and after due consideration several times declared and confirmed in writing that he no longer wants to live and has requested that he be helped to die in a dignified way, after more than one conversation with him and after he has sought the opinion of a second doctor, may end his life,' i.e. may kill him. 'May kill him' sounds gruesome. Nonetheless this is what euthanasia really means. It is essentially a form of self-killing with the help of another. The crucial ethical question therefore is: does man have the right to end his life? In religious parlance: is self-killing a sin or not? Whether the cooperation of the doctor is ethically permitted or not depends on the answer to this question.

One hears two contrasting answers to this question. Modern humanism acknowledges the right to choose death, provided the legal conditions are observed. It wants to enable a dignified end to a person's life, which means a death without fear and pain and in clear consciousness. By contrast, the Church authorities and all who follow them in this condemn suicide and therefore also euthanasia. In the words of John-Paul II they call this 'a culture of death'. Ever since, the Church authorities like to use this degrading expression. Of course, the different stances are connected with the differences in worldviews.

Critical analysis of the non-believing modern humanist view

Modern humanism is based on the affirmation of the autonomy of the cosmos and of man. The norms for good and evil are to be sought in the essence of man and not in a supernatural world. What is good and worthy of man, is that which leads him to a richer degree of humanity, liberates him, encourages him and promotes his human growth. What is bad by contrast is everything that constrains him, alarms him, degrades him, makes him dependent and keeps him immature, or meaninglessly tortures him and thus casts a shadow over his life. But one of the fundamental ideas of modernity is also that man has inalienable rights, the first among them being a right to life and to physical integrity. No one is allowed to take these precious things from him against his will. But he has the right, of his own free will, to opt out of life and therefore to commit suicide. He has this right on the basis of his freedom, which is the concrete form of his autonomy. For what does autonomy mean, if a person is not free to decide on his actions, even the action which puts an end to his life?

Non-believing modernity, therefore, begins with the premise of human autonomy but unfortunately sees it mainly from a negative angle as a denial of any power outside the cosmos which would decide, according to its own wisdom, what we are allowed to do and what not. The one-sidedness of this view has a foundation in history. The affirmation of human autonomy had to assert itself against the tough opposition of the dominant heteronomous notions. From the beginning it met with the hostility of the traditionalist camp and therefore built up in response a kind of aggressiveness against this camp. This aggressiveness leads to the spontaneous suspicion that the opponents of euthanasia are not being led by care for human values and for a humanly dignified death, but by Church prescriptions coming ultimately from an imaginary God-in-Heaven who would decide at his own discretion what we are allowed to do and what not. Such a God would simply be the denial of the human autonomy. Here modern humanism mounts the barricades. This aggressiveness also explains its attempts to extend the immunity from prosecution of euthanasia to include children and sufferers from dementia. But autonomy should not be seen first and foremost as a denial, as a rejection of heteronomy. It is primarily something positive, the acknowledgement, namely, that man is to take hold of his own life and to seek and find the way in which he can live a life that is worthy of a human being. For this he has to know his own essence, know who he is, in the spirit of the words written on the gable of the temple of Apollo in Delphi: 'gnoothi sauton, learn to know yourself'. And what will this self-knowledge teach him? That he is essentially a fellow human being, a member of an infinitely large family. He is autonomous only as part of the human family. But belonging to a whole means being essentially dependent on the whole. Thus the individual's autonomy is not unlimited autonomy. In his decision about departing from life he should also consider the good of his fellow men. This duty is all the more binding the closer his bond to them. To be allowed to choose death he should be able to offer a convincing reason. Non-believing modernity realizes this as well and in this way implicitly modifies the initially general affirmation of the right to commit suicide. But the importance of this duty to be account-able to the totality does not come through loud enough.

Convincing reasons for choosing suicide are given by the Stoic Seneca in one of his letters to Lucilius. There he writes: 'If one kind of dying is connected with torture while the other is simple and easy, why should one not take the second option?' And he gives two or three examples. Also at the end of Malraux's *La condition humaine* we also find such an example: three communist revolutionaries have fallen into the hands of the Kwomintang. They know what their enemies will do with them: shove them alive into the furnace of a locomotive. The senior of the three has a potassium cyanide tablet. He breaks it into two pieces and gives one to each of his terrified comrades who use them to take their lives. Not only non-religious modernity will fully approve of this suicide; the defenders of tradition will also approve, although they are thereby unconsciously undermining their thesis that suicide is murder. One can multiply at will the number of such cases, which should not necessarily be concerned only with physical torture. Psychological suffering can become unbearable for someone and be a reason for choosing suicide.

Naturally one can always question whether the pain from which one wants to escape is great enough to justify such a decision ethically. But by its very nature the answer to this question is subjective, i.e. dependent on the person who is making the choice. A Socrates will, with regard to the duty of enduring pain, set the bar much higher than someone who has always been led by the maxims of consumer society. But, as the saying goes, it is easy to spend another person's money. We should not demand bravery of others which we are not sure we could manage ourselves. This applies especially to Church authorities who, without having the slightest notion of what others have to undergo, speak of 'a culture of death' when people undergoing unbearable suffering beg for euthanasia. Out of respect for life, as they say.

A second and basically even fuller justification for suicide is acknowledged not only by modernity but also by traditional believers: dedication to the life and wellbeing of one's fellow man. With regard to Maximilian Kolbe's decision to take the place of a co-prisoner and go down into the execution bunker, can one speak of suicide? We should think of the words attributed to Jesus that the greatest proof of love is to lay down one's life for one's friends. And we should think even more of the fact that he did this himself. For he could have fled, but he obviously decided that this would be a kind of infidelity to his fellow men. This seems to lead us far away from the euthanasia debate. But this is not the case. It shows that suicide in whatever form is not to be condemned always and everywhere.

Witnesses of a freely chosen and well-prepared euthanasia (as is possible in Benelux countries) confirm that it is really possible to speak of a 'good death', that euthanasia, contrary to the statements of the traditional camp, does not necessarily need to have a negative effect on human dignity in death but can even enhance it. Euthanasia does not need to be 'a culture of death' (though it can be and often is) but can be instrumental in achieving a 'good death'. A witness to such a death writes: 'I noticed that people can cope with life longer when they know that at a moment of their choice they can say: I've had enough.' Such witnesses make it plausible that euthanasia can serve to ensure human dignity in a person's death. For modernity such a plea is not necessary. But it is useful for the criticism of the Church's standpoint which now follows.

Critical analysis of the views of the traditional believer

As was said at the beginning, pre-modern believers expressly condemn euthanasia and speak of suicide assisted by someone. The assistant thereby makes himself an accessory to murder. The charter of the Council of Europe of 1998 says the same: 'Respect for the dignity of the dying person can never approve of intentional killing procedures. The expressed wish to die is not a sufficient basis for justifying it.' It is not that the Council of Europe is particularly inspired by the Church. But its explanation shows at least that even in modern Europe there is still unease about euthanasia, which comes from the past and which has not yet been critically analysed.

This unease is mostly explained as an innate human prohibition against killing a fellow man. We are free to kill animals. That is not murder. Only killing a person in a free and conscious act and for base motives can be called murder. But if we look further into this prohibition against killing and ask who could have written this law in us, it becomes clear what the traditional believer has in mind, namely an extra-cosmic law-giving authority. The usual formulation of the prohibition reveals this: 'Thou shalt not kill.' It comes straight out of the Book of Exodus in which it appears as one of the Ten Commandments. If it did not come from there, the formulation would be instead: 'It is not permissible to kill anyone' or 'You should have great respect for the life of your fellow men'. The words from the Bible count as a decisive argument which is absolutely binding, because of the divine and infallible character attributed in the heteronomous view to words from the Bible. Another, related argument goes: 'We did not give ourselves life and therefore it is not ours to dispose of.' But what I have received as a gift is my property, it belongs only to me, and it is at my disposal. Besides, we did not give life to the animals and yet we are allowed to slaughter them. It is clear how with such arguments one can become tied up in contradictions.

Furthermore, this commandment like every law needs interpretation: concretely, what comes under this law and what does not? That is for the law-giver to clarify. But the divine law-giver is not accessible. We are forced to find this out for ourselves from what he has ordered and forbidden elsewhere. And what do we find then? Soon after this 'Thou shalt not kill' the same law-giver for Israel gives the command to wipe out the whole Midianite people. And in the Book of Josue he commands that all the cities of Canaan be conquered and that all that live there be slaughtered. The fifth commandment refers, therefore, only to the killing of fellow Jews. All others are fair game. Besides, the same law-giver demands the death penalty for all kinds of infringements of his laws, committed by the Jews themselves. Thus also this kind of killing does not come under that commandment. Ultimately it only concerns the arbitrary killing of another Jew. In other words: murder of a member of one's tribe. The German Ecumenical Bible Translation has rightly instead of 'Thou shalt not kill', 'Thou shalt not murder'. Murder belongs to the category of what is ethically reprehensible; it always includes guilt because the perpetrator consciously refuses someone his right to live. As a rule it has to do with the satisfying of some passion like hatred, lust, envy, ill-will, denial of the value of a fellow man, briefly: lack of love. But if the killing is an expression of humaneness and sympathy, a sign of true care and love for a fellow man, what then? Or is that perhaps not possible? It is possible with a house pet which one has loved and would dearly want to keep alive, but which is suffering too much. When one can no longer do anything more to help it, (with 'death in one's heart') one has the vet put it to sleep. In Milan Kundera's novel *The Unbearable Lightness of Being* the euthanasia of a dog is so poignantly portrayed that tears come into one's eyes. Why should it be a crime in the case of a deeply loved person who is suffering greatly and asks for the relief of an injection? There is no way that this euthanasia can be called murder. There is no trace of evil intention, self-seeking, lack of love. The commandment which concerns murder cannot be called on in this case.

The Latin word *suicidium*, literally self-killing, has been translated in German-speaking countries as self-murder and is therefore automatically seen as a crime. This translation reflects the way the Church, also in other than German-speaking countries, always thinks about self-killing and also explains why it punished self-killing with the refusal of a Church burial and did not allow burial in consecrated ground. The person's last act was murder and therefore a mortal sin, and he was not able to show any sign of repentance.

But within half a century the earlier attitude towards suicide has, at least in the Church, changed considerably. Suicide is now excused rather than condemned. Understanding and sympathy now set the tone. It is true that people prefer to cover up suicide. This is probably an after-effect of earlier condemnation. In a death notice we will never read: 'Mr and Mrs X-Y report with great sorrow that on 10 May their beloved Kurt took his own life.' In practice, the parishes do not follow the Church burial directives. We have become more aware of how a person who takes his life must have felt. His will to live was not equal to the appalling psychological or physical suffering he was enduring. Death was his only escape.

For the condemnation of suicide the Church tradition can no longer invoke its decisive source, the Bible. In the First Book of

Samuel 31:4-5 there is, without any criticism, the story of the suicide of King Saul, who uses it as a means to escape degrading treatment at the hands of the victorious Philistines; or in Judges 16:30 the suicide of Samson, which is reminiscent of today's suicide assassinations. Tradition also leaves the door slightly ajar. Indeed, several fathers of the Church found that to protect her virginity a girl could throw herself down to her death. Ultimately the traditional view is not so very different from the modern one. Where there are serious grounds, suicide ceases to be ethically reprehensible. But if this is the case a global condemnation of euthanasia is not sustainable, for it is a kind of aided suicide. Therefore such a prohibition for want of biblical support loses its foundation also for pre-modern believers. For modernity it had long since lost its foundation because of its heteronomous nature.

Does the prohibition perhaps find a more reliable foundation in the Hippocratic oath? By this oath the doctor swears to do all in his power to serve the life and health of his fellow human beings. It is of no great importance that this oath, in spite of what age-old tradition says, does not stem from Hippocrates. But it is important that God-in-Heaven, and therefore the absolute, no longer plays a role in swearing oaths today. What is left of oaths is only a solemn promise and, because of human limitations and the interim status, such a promise cannot be absolutely binding. There can be circumstances where the relevance of the Hippocratic oath of the doctor ends. For example, when even the best palliative care can no longer result in a humanly dignified death and the pain and deterioration cannot be ended without recourse to a lethal injection.

The fundamental criticism of the Church's prohibition of euthanasia can be further reinforced by the following considerations. One often hears the comment after a person's long and painful death that death was truly a deliverance for the deceased. Why should we not have the right to hasten this deliverance, provided that the dying person asks for it himself? And has the Church ever condemned hunger strikes? A hunger strike is in fact a threat of suicide and is even the beginning of suicide. The opponents of euthanasia also maintain that their motive is the genuine concern for a dignified human death. But there are enough cases in which this waiting for a death (according to God's plan?) is inhumane and therefore lacking in human dignity. In his book *Dying with Human Dignity* Hans Küng talks about his brother, a young man of twenty-two years whose brain tumour could not be treated successfully with radiation, chemotherapy and surgery, so that one organ after another was attacked. The slow process of dying led for days to a horrible struggling for breath, all in full consciousness, until the water rising into his lungs finally brought on his death. And Küng asks: 'Is that what God really wanted?'

The opponents of euthanasia say against this that we should let nature take its course and even in such cases we should not interfere with the natural process of dying, even when the dying person asks us to. But on what do they base this statement? And who is this 'nature' whose handiwork we are not to interfere with and who could command us to wait passively for a horrible death? Probably a God-in-Heaven in disguise. Has this God really, from all eternity, determined the minute of our dying and the extent of our suffering? And why do we not let nature take its course when a tumour is found or when someone collapses with a heart attack? In these cases we act immediately. Perhaps it is even more contradictory that precisely those who with the letter to the Philippians 1:21 are to see death as gain and the beginning of eternal joy, would yet like to delay this gain as long as possible and not allow us to bring forward slightly our entrance into the longed-for eternal joy. The Muslim suicide bombers are much more logical in their 'faith'.

Palliative medicine

That may be enough by way of criticism of the Church's prohibition of euthanasia. Fortunately, pre-modern believers do more than just reject euthanasia. With great commitment they support palliative care. Experience teaches us namely that a request for euthanasia is often only masking the desire to be able to live on but without unnecessary pain. Modern medicine makes it largely possible to satisfy this desire. Where there is excellent palliative care the request for euthanasia usually (not always!) disappears. That is why palliative care is to be preferred to euthanasia. Traditional believers agree to this, thus proving that it does really want the best for the mortally ill person, namely a humanly dignified end to life, 'a good death'. Their thinking and acting is based precisely on their Christian background and this background gives them a clear advantage over non-believing modernity, for the good of humanity is to be sought more in the exercise of love for our fellow men than in the exercise of autonomy. Therefore as death approaches the attentive care and constant closeness of the professional or voluntary carers and friends are much more of a blessing than a euthanasia law, no matter how good it is. Despite its loud claims to being the advocate of dying people, modern humanism seems to have no other answer to the mortal anguish than euthanasia. What contributes to this is probably that their opponents give the (not always false) impression that suffering is sent by God and that he wants the person to wait patiently for the end of life that he has decreed. Humanism's answer can be compared to the temporary exits for trucks descending onto the Brenner autobahn. If the brakes threaten to fail, the trucks can gradually be brought to a stop on these rising exits. The normal 'exit', however, is palliative medicine.

But this is not a cure-all. Its motto is indeed 'put more life into the days' and provides them precisely with what most of them want, even when they ask for euthanasia. But what if this goal cannot be attained and the suffering person, despite the best palliative care, still asks for help to die? Is it respecting his autonomy (and if I do not respect this I am not respecting him as a human being) not to take his decision seriously and to say: 'You want to die, but I don't want you to, and I know better than you what is good for you'? That is pure paternalism. Palliative medicine has reached its limits here and should make room for euthanasia.

Furthermore, excellent palliative care requires a warm human infrastructure and considerable investment. First, the infrastructure. On the basis of the advanced ageing of the population the number of people in need of this care is increasing incessantly. But the supply of well-trained and committed carers is not keeping pace. The numbers are diminishing. This is not surprising. In a society geared to profit and consumption we cannot expect that enough helpers will generously take on this unattractive service. For this reason only some of those in need of this excellent care can hope to have it. And what happens to the others? Added to this infrastructural problem is the problem of investment. The following question will serve to anticipate protests raised against this seemingly materialistic approach. If in a lifeboat there is room for 20 people at the most and the boat is already full, what is to happen when a further 20 drowning people are begging for a place? The investment possibilities of a society are likewise limited. A state's financial cake has to be divided up in a reasonable way between many necessary services in order of importance. The ever increasing number of old patients in need of care will multiply the cost of palliative care. But the cost can only grow to a certain level, otherwise there is no longer anything left for other often more important services. Palliative care then threatens to become a hardly affordable luxury. A rich person will perhaps be able to meet the cost himself. But are we then, with a heavy heart, to deliver over the others to an end of life that is no longer humanly dignified? It is the same painful problem as the one concerning the already overfilled lifeboat. To be readier to meet the request for euthanasia could relieve the problem a little. But raising awareness of the problems connected with palliative medicine has its dangerous side. It could arouse fear in those who need care that people would prefer that they did not live too long so that room would become free for others.

Traditional believers would not see it as euthanasia to give a suffering patient large doses of medication which dull their consciousness even though it has the unintended effect of hastening the process of dying through paralysis of the respiratory muscles. They attempt to justify such a treatment by application of the principle of double effect. One intends a praiseworthy effect, the alleviation of pain, and not the other effect, which is death. But unfortunately death possibly follows from the alleviation of pain. In Chapter Four another solution was put forward, based on the knowledge that no single act is completely good or completely bad. Every act is a mixture of both. One should always honestly ask which of the two in a concrete case has the more weight. If one considers the end of one's suffering as the greater good (or a lesser evil) than the continuation of the pain or continuation of life in a half-conscious state and being a burden to others, it is then an ethically responsible decision to choose that greater good (or lesser evil). Weighing up the good and bad sides can therefore lead to euthanasia and thus this view departs considerably from traditional notions which stigmatize euthanasia as the 'culture of death'.

If the suffering person is no longer in a position to express his wishes we have landed in a grey area. If he or she has made a formal advance decision, the law in Benelux countries allows euthanasia. If this law is ethically acceptable (something the pre-modern view must condemn as a violation of the biblical commandment of God), euthanasia is also ethically acceptable when someone without making a formal advance decision has often expressed his wish to die, in complaints like: 'The good Lord has forgotten me' or 'I pray every day that the good Lord will take me'. But there is always the condition that one is not led by self-interest but by genuine care for the suffering person.

But what if the mortally sick person has never said anything of this kind? Here we are totally in the grey zone, as in the following case. A very old man lying in a coma is artificially fed over a period of months but shows no reactions at all so that it is not possible to know whether he hears or knows anything anymore. It costs society an enormous amount of money, that is no benefit to him other than the continuation of his vegetative – not even human – life, and this money is thereby not available for socially more worthy causes. And what does anyone gain by living a few months longer, not as a person to communicate with, not as a partner to encounter but only as a burden not just to himself but also to his fellow human beings? It is not one of our duties to be a burden to others. Our duty is the opposite: to carry the burden of others. Precisely this duty summons us to care for the dying, those suffering from dementia, and Alzheimer patients. But the traditional view condemns euthanasia so completely, that it considers it a crime even to stop artificial feeding or breathing of a sick person living in a persistent vegetative state as did Eluana Englaro or the old man just mentioned. And the turning off of machines is not even euthanasia. Of course, in the traditional view, genuine euthanasia in this grey zone is simply out of the question.

The view of the modern believer

This view shares with modernity the recognition of human autonomy. It therefore denies our dependence on a 'second world' which lays down laws, and it acknowledges the right and the duty of man to decide for himself what he has to do and has not to do. With regard to the end of his life it acknowledges his right to deal with it himself, but emphasizes much more strongly than the non-believing humanist the duty to heed the good of one's fellow men. If suicide is to be ethically acceptable the decision must be able to produce good reasons. It should either be the means to escape from suffering that has become unbearable or it should serve a greater good, as in the case of Maximilian Kolbe. This duty makes it clear that human autonomy is in the eyes of the modern believer not absolute autonomy.

It is not absolute autonomy above all for the reason that it is a shared autonomy and therefore dependent. As a form of autonomy it is a manifestation of an infinitely greater autonomy. With pre-modern faith the modern believer shares a belief in a transcendent fundamental reality which embraces all things. But in contrast to the pre-modern faith it does not see this reality as an almighty creator outside and above the cosmos but as the Fundamental Love which produces everything and which in the developing cosmos takes on an ever clearer shape. The evolutionary drive in the cosmos in which this Fundamental Love reveals itself translates itself in our autonomous being into the duty to increase in sympathy and empathy and care. When it concerns dying, the modern believer stresses in agreement with the pre-modern believer and much more strongly than modern humanism, the value of palliative care, which with modern medicine makes it possible for dying to be as humanly dignified as possible. Humanly dignified here means a death with as little pain as possible and with the highest possible level of consciousness. And the second part is important, for the more the consciousness is dulled the more the person is incapable of engaging with his fellow men and with the source of his life, the Fundamental Love. And precisely that is his essential task. For this reason one can also ask why inducing an irreversible coma should be preferred to euthanasia, as it is in the pre-modern view.

The view of the modern believer does not forget the two limits to palliative care described above and which the traditional view takes too little into consideration: the threat of a lack of well-trained, committed carers and the money trap. But where palliative care reaches its material limits a humanly dignified death should be brought about in a different way.

But there is a further limit, and this lies within the suffering person. Even the best of care is not always able to provide a humanly dignified way of dying. It often happens that the sufferer is not able to carry out and persevere in his duty to be there for others. Assuming that he was ever aware of this duty. The pre-modern conception with its recourse to supernatural ideas as a rule no longer offers him a way out. By contrast, modern medicine does offer him a way out: euthanasia. To characterize this as proof of a culture of death shows a lack of understanding of the terrible hopelessness in the person who is asking for euthanasia.

The modern believer can reconcile himself to the fact that someone, for want of another means of escaping from suffering, chooses euthanasia, even when this suffering does not yet amount to mortal anguish. If he were still healthy enough to make this step without help, he could commit suicide. But this is precisely what the suffering, bed-ridden person in need of care is no longer able to do. He needs help. He needs a doctor who knows how it is to be done and who is also prepared to do it, and who will do it out of pure humanity. Only then is aid for suicide (as the organization *Dignitate* in Switzerland offers) or euthanasia (as approved by Belgian and Dutch law) not unethical. Only what is done out of love for the sufferer is good. But then also everything that is done out of love, is good. Even where it is not a question of unbearable suffering, which Belgian law lays down as a condition, it seems acceptable to give up a place in the lifeboat of palliative care in favour of another person. Then he is acting, to use the expression of the Latin poet Horace, like a *conviva satur*, a replete guest who gratefully stands up from the table of life so that another can sit down at this table for a while longer.

But what does the modern believer say regarding the grey zone cases mentioned above when the person is no longer in a position to express his own will? The modern believer then tends towards the modern rather than to the traditional view. He is inclined to think that one can help someone, precisely because one genuinely loves him (always an essential condition and justification) with the life-shortening means he needs to escape from a condition which is no longer humanly dignified: from incontinence, bedsores, respiratory distress, dehydration. He accepts this all the more readily when the suffering person has

made it known through an advance decision or through other
earlier indications that he wants to be liberated from a situation
of total dependency and need for help in which he might find
himself. In contrast to the traditional believer the modern
believer has no ethical problems with this form of liberation from
suffering. But can he also find it acceptable when the sick person
who has now fallen into unconsciousness and whom one loves,
such as one's own mother, one's father, has never said anything
about euthanasia? Then he should take a long look at the beloved
person and ask himself what he would wish for himself in such a
situation. And take also into consideration the burden which this
wretched situation imposes on many others, without a genuinely
human encounter being possible for the sick person. It is, of
course, inevitable that people are (also) a burden to one another.
But the fact that something is inevitable does not necessarily
mean that it is good and praiseworthy and that one should not
try to spare others this inevitable burden.

Furthermore, we should consider that a person in an irreversible coma is not deprived by euthanasia of any genuine human
life, but only from a last vestige of vegetative life. Genuine human
life consists in the possibility of being a person for others. This
possibility no longer exists for a person lying there in an
irreversible coma. The ethical assessment of how we act in this
totally grey zone, depends on the genuineness and honesty of the
love one has for the person concerned. Genuine love justifies
both things: the palliative care which tries, out of reverence, to
prolong for a while the vegetative (or also animal) life which is
left of the person's truly human life; and the decision to
terminate through euthanasia what is in fact a condition un-
worthy of a human being. This euthanasia rests on the rightly
surmised wish of the beloved person who is lying in a coma. It is
evident this can never be approved of by a law. All too often in
our materialistically oriented society the requisite love and
selflessness are lacking. A flood of abuses would result. It does
often happen in hospitals and care homes, but secretly and
usually not out of love and care for the person whose life is
hastily brought to an end. But this abuse does not take away the
ethical defensibility of such an act.

Perhaps these reflections can bridge the gulf between the two
opposing positions, both of which are dictated by care and
respect for the sick person. They can free the traditional

approach to the problem from the heteronomous fear which unconsciously plays a big part in the condemnation of euthanasia. They can also open the eyes of their modern humanist opponents to the excellence of palliative medicine, which mobilizes much more human goodness and commitment than is the case with assisted suicide. Modern humanism, moreover, should free itself from the almost morbid tendency to say no, when traditional believers say yes, and should look more honestly for what best serves human dignity in living and in dying.

EPILOGUE

It is a truly extraordinary phenomenon. The mediaeval, renaissance and baroque periods were epochs when culture flourished and wonderful works of art were created, thereby suggesting a high level of human quality, and they were penetrated as well by a religion with high ethical claims. Yet within these periods deep and dark abysses of inhumanity were unlocked. There were no objections to slavery and the slave trade flourished, wars were continually waged in which the soldiery had free rein, prisons were horrendous, Jews were considered fair game and were again and again victims of pogroms, robberies and murder, torture was a legal means to force confessions from the guilty and innocent alike, ideas regarding faith which seemed to contradict the currently held views could be enough to have a person arrested and executed. But not only was the death penalty quite common, it was often even carried out with great cruelty as a kind of popular entertainment, as on the wheel or at the stake. And that is only a selection from a much greater whole. How was that possible in a culture in which the gospel was read out every Sunday and was acknowledged as authoritative? Is there not on every page a call to sympathetic humanity? And what is the origin of the surprisingly rapid change from the 18th century on? Only two hundred years later everything is different, and we are annoyed and disgusted at the thought that things used to be like that.

The change began with the fact that the 18th century gave birth to a new way of looking at reality, a new worldview. We call it modernity, and its root is the Enlightenment. In earlier times religion dictated the worldview. In the West it was Christianity. The Enlightenment knocked the then dominant religion off its throne by bidding farewell to God-in-Heaven. What brought them to this step was the new insight which came with scientific discoveries. Confronted by the inexplicable and often frightening aspects of many natural phenomena, man had seen in them extra-mundane, supernatural powers at work, to which he gave the name of gods. In this way the concept of 'gods', later of a sole God, became firmly established and no one would dream of doubting his existence and his power. But the development of the sciences which began in the 16th century and gathered ever more strength, made a supernatural explanation superfluous, at first for some natural phenomena, and gradually for all phenomena. With the Enlightenment the very slow death of God in the psyche of Western man had its beginning. Since there was now a natural explanation for everything, there was no longer any need for an active and intervening God. Everything ran smoothly without him. He was no longer encountered anywhere and so he gradually disappeared into oblivion. He had become ineffective. Soon he would be unreal.

But God-in-Heaven had always been the law-giver and punisher, and life was ordered and determined by his laws. His death had to bring about chaos in the world, unless man looked elsewhere for the laws needed for living. And just as he had sought and found the laws which govern the course of things in nature, he sought and found ethical laws in his own being. He discovered that he was called to become ever more humane and caring. And it became clear to him that many laws and bans that came from supposedly divine instances were no longer valid. The end of religion thus meant the beginning of a new ethic.

Was the Christian religion therefore guilty of an earlier lack of humanity? On the contrary. Its sacred books called for love of our neighbour, even for love of our enemies. In this way it had become the source of care for the poor and the suffering, which did not exist anywhere else. The names of the pioneers of that care would fill a book. Modern society has acknowledged the importance of this work, in the long run, by taking on this care. And that not religion was to blame for the earlier inhumanity is clearly seen where atheistic humanism became the leading ideology. Liberty, equality, fraternity had been the slogan of the French Revolution. Just three years later Robespierre ruled in Paris every day the heads of his opponents rolled under the guillotine. But that was chicken feed by comparison with the contempt for humanity which would soon manifest itself in the atheist regimes: in Bolshevism with its gulags, in Nazism with its concentration camps, in Maoism with its cultural revolution, in the murderous tyranny of Pol Pot or in unbridled capitalism which mercilessly exploits the helpless and makes the poor ever poorer. No matter how much one tries to explain the evil in human history, it remains inexplicable. But one thing is clear: it will take a long, long time before the human race emerges from its animal prehistory which reveals itself in evil. It is still on the way. It is still nothing more than a missing link between the hominid and true man.

Therefore, a 'not guilty' for religion. Compared with atheistic humanism, religion can also put forward the additional proof of innocence that through the acknowledgement of a supreme authority it protects man from the overweening pride which shows its face in contempt for others. But the religions, the Christian religion as well, have not only given this highest authority anthropomorphic features but in doing so they have also broadly copied the model of the rulers they knew. And these had human faults: they promoted submissiveness, abused their power, were vengeful, often cruel, could always be bought and accepted no responsibility towards their subjects. Much of this found its way imperceptibly into the image of the celestial rulers – even into the image of God-in-Heaven. This notion of God functioned as a kind of heavenly canopy stretched over the injustice and cruelty of his worshippers, and piously covered over these crimes. And it was not too difficult to find in the gospels, and still less difficult to find in the Old Testament – both of which were seen as collections of God's own words – here and there a sentence which more or less justified the evil and made it acceptable.

With the collapse of religion in Western society this celestial canopy was also in ribbons, and all that it covered over appeared loathsome in the naked light of day. Thus a new ethics developed, which distanced itself on some important points from the pre-modern ethics based on religion. It is true that the Church authorities still reject modernity, because it proclaims human autonomy and therefore no longer accepts a God-in-Heaven reigning over the cosmos. However, in the last two centuries they have secretly smuggled much of modern ethics into their own. They, too, now energetically condemn slavery, torture, the death penalty, hatred of Jews, war, religious intolerance – all things which in the past they were eager to practise and justify. Now the Church praises democracy, freedom of conscience and of religion and human rights, which it used to condemn no less vigorously than Islam is still doing. Nevertheless, something still remains of what it used to justify earlier as the will of God. This applies especially to its sexual ethics, its economic ethics and its bioethics. These points have been addressed in the book and corrected in terms of modernity.

But neither is modern ethics, for its part, without errors. The inhumanity which atheist modernity has produced points to the active presence of evil in its roots. And it lacks the model of humanity and love that the Christian has in Jesus. From him the Christian learns that God is love. Indeed, the traditional name 'God' no longer means for him, as a modern Christian, the anthropomorphic God-in-Heaven but the Fundamental Mystery, its continually growing self-expression. And since for a believing Christian the essence of this creative Fundamental Mystery is love, not understood as a heart-warming feeling but as radiation, as emanation, it unceasingly drives man to go out of himself and to turn towards his fellow human beings. This exodus from the self becomes the norm for ethical behaviour. Good is therefore no longer what corresponds to tradition or custom or divine law, but that which is born of clear-sighted love. With the ethics of the modern believer developed in this book the author has tried to link the good of the past with the good in modernity. It is up to the reader to decide how far he has succeeded.